Causes

NANCY DUFRESNE

Ed Dufresne Ministries
Murrieta, California

Causes
ISBN: 978-0-94076-327-2
Copyright © 2009 by Ed Dufresne Ministries
P.O. Box 1010
Murrieta, CA 92564
U.S.A.

Published by Ed Dufresne Ministries
P.O. Box 1010
Murrieta, CA 92564
U.S.A.

www.eddufresne.org

Contents

Chapter 1

UNDER THE BLESSING, NOT THE CURSE

Galatians 3:13 & 14
13 CHRIST HATH REDEEMED US FROM THE CURSE OF THE LAW, being made a curse for us: for it is written, Cursed is every one that hangeth on a tree:
14 That the blessing of Abraham might come on the Gentiles through Jesus Christ; that we might receive the promise of the Spirit through faith.

What is the curse of the law? Deuteronomy 28:1-14 lists the blessings that would come on those who obeyed God's Word, but Deuteronomy 28:15-68 lists the curses that would come on those who failed to obey God's law. God's will was that His people live under the blessing and not the curse. But when God's people broke His commandments, they no longer were under His divine protection. All He could do was permit the devil to bring those afflictions upon them. Their sin and wrongdoing brought those dreadful curses upon them. God didn't commission these curses to come on the people, but He had to permit them because of their disobedience.

The curse of the law is three-fold: spiritual death (spiritual death is separation from God), sickness, and poverty. But Christ has redeemed us from the curse of the law!

How did He do that? He was made a curse for us. He took our place in the curse. The curse that belonged to you and me, He took upon Himself. The curse that fell upon us, He took upon Himself.

When did He take the curse? *"...Cursed is everyone that hangeth on a tree."* He took the curse when He hung on the tree at Calvary.

Why did He take our place in the curse? *"That the BLESSING of Abraham might come on the Gentiles...."* He took the curse from us so that we could live under the blessing and be free from the curse.

Jesus took our place in the three-fold curse:

1. Jesus took our place in spiritual death (which is separation from the presence of God). He was separated from the presence of the Father when He went to hell, paying the price for our sin. He freed us from our fallen sin nature and gave us a new nature. Now we have God's nature in us. Now we can approach the Father and live in His presence.

We'll never again be separated from the Father. We'll never again be separated from all that He is. We'll never again be separated from God's love, God's wisdom, God's ability, God's strength, or from answers.

2. Jesus took our place in sickness. The stripes that purchased our healing were laid on Him so that we could be whole.

We'll never again be separated from health. Healing is in us because the Healer is in us.

3. Jesus took our place in poverty and lack. At Calvary poverty was laid on Him, for Second Corinthians 8:9 tells us, *"...though he was rich, yet for your sakes HE BECAME POOR, THAT YE THROUGH HIS POVERTY MIGHT BE RICH."* To be rich means to have a full supply. He took our place in poverty so that we would have a full supply.

We'll never again be separated from supply, for Philippians 4:19 tells us, *"But my God shall SUPPLY all your need according to his riches in glory by Christ Jesus."*

He took our place in the three-fold curse so that we would be free from the curse, and live under the blessing.

Don't Give Place to the Devil

Because the unbeliever is in rebellion to God's Word, he has no protection from the curse. The unbeliever is subject to the curse: spiritual death, sickness and poverty. Because he's under the curse, he has sickness, financial problems, wayward children, tragedies, crises and a host of other problems.

But Christ has redeemed and freed His children from the lordship of the curse because Galatians 3:13 tells us, *"Christ hath redeemed us from the curse of the law...."* No one who is born again is still under the lordship of Satan or the curse.

Since that is true, then why do Christians experience sickness, financial crisis, failures, tragedies, and other problems? It's not because of the same reason unbelievers face these problems. Unbelievers have these problems because they are under the curse. But believers are free from the curse, so why would believers face some of these same difficulties? Ephesians 4:27 tells us why. *"Neither give place to the devil."* Believers face difficulties unnecessarily because they give place to the devil.

Notice that Ephesians 4:27 says, *"Neither GIVE place to the devil."* He can't take a place in you; you have to give him a place. You can open the door to the devil. The devil can't do anything to you anytime he wants to. If he could, then why would he have to deceive you first? Satan is the deceiver. He has to deceive you into believing the wrong thing before he can work the wrong thing in your life. He can't take a place in your life unless you give him a place by opening the door to him.

If you can give place to the devil, and open the door to him to gain access to your life, then you can take place back from the devil by closing the door to him and ridding him of access to your life.

It's to be understood, however, that just because you may be facing a test or a trial, doesn't mean that you're failing, and it doesn't mean you've opened the door to the devil. Even when you're in the will of God, the enemy is going to attack you. Difficulties are going to come your way because the devil seeks to hinder your progress in God's plan for your life.

It's one thing to be attacked because you're progressing in God's plan, but it's another thing entirely to open yourself up to an attack of the enemy because of disobedience to God's Word.

Even if you do miss God and open yourself up to an attack, if you will judge yourself and repent, making the needed changes, you can receive victory and come out of that difficulty.

To be "tested" and to "fail" are two different things. The enemy will attack and test you, but victory belongs to you every time, so the test shouldn't result in failure. But if there is failure, there's a cause.

"For This Cause..."

First Corinthians 11:30 reads, *"For this CAUSE many are weak and sickly among you, and many sleep (die prematurely)."* This verse shows us that there's a cause when Christians fail. There's a cause when Christians are weak, or sickly, or die prematurely; they've given place to the devil somewhere. This verse also shows us a progression: first, weakness, which then moves into sickness, and then sickness can move to premature death. When there's weakness, let's stop it before it moves to the next stage of sickness. Let's not allow it to progress too far before we start examining where the cause is and make needed corrections.

Get It Closed

Now, if we do open the door to the enemy to attack us, then we're going to have to close the door before we can receive our help. If we opened the door to sickness, then we're going to have to close that door before we can receive healing. If we opened the door to the enemy to attack us financially, then we're going to have to close that door before we can receive our supply. If we opened the door to any difficulty, then we're going to have to close that door before we can receive our needed help. It's not that God withholds our help from us, but we are unable to receive the help He gives us when we fail to close the door to the enemy.

If there is a failure to receive in someone's life, it's never on God's side, it's always on man's side.

No Condemnation

The devil will seek to get us under condemnation, and will accuse us saying that because we missed God and opened the door to any difficulties, that we have to accept a measure of defeat for it. But that's not true. If we repent and make the necessary changes to walk in line with God's will, we don't have to accept even the smallest measure of defeat or condemnation.

Even if you do miss God and don't realize it, you have the Holy Spirit who will enlighten you. When the Holy Spirit enlightens you about a place where you may have missed it and sinned, it lifts you up, it doesn't put you down.

When the devil accuses you of where you may have missed it and sinned, it puts you down under guilt, fear, and condemnation.

Even if you did miss it, God's not using the devil to reveal it to you. God will instruct and correct you in a way that builds you up. Anything that puts you down, accuses you, makes you feel down and depressed is of the devil, and is to be rejected.

Making Your Spirit Sensitive

If you opened the door to the devil, but don't know where, you can ask God and He will show you. When looking to the Lord to show you, you may need to take some extra time to pray in other tongues. By praying in tongues, you make your spirit sensitive to the Holy Spirit, and then you can hear what the Spirit says to you. For those whose spirits aren't sensitive to the Holy Spirit, it may take them a while of speaking in tongues before their spirits are sensitive enough to hear.

As a pastor, I have found that if one of my congregation members is facing a great difficulty because they have opened the door to the devil, by praying in tongues regarding their situation, many times God will show me where they opened the door to the devil. He shows me that so that I can help them.

God's best belongs to all of His people, but experiencing His best requires obedience to His Word so that we don't give place to the devil. When we fail to do the Word, we give place to the devil. But when we act on God's Word, we give place to God and His blessings.

Chapter 2

CAUSE #1 - LOSS OF PEACE

My husband was conducting a miracle service at our church in Murrieta, California, where he had taught on the subject of divine healing. At the end of his sermon he turned to me and said, "Do you have something by the Holy Ghost?" I've learned that when he asks that, it usually means I have something God wants me to do, so I just got up, not knowing what I would do next.

I took the microphone and began to speak in other tongues, then I interpreted what I said into English. This happened three times. What the Spirit spoke through me was giving us three primary ways sickness enters the life of the believer.

Since Christians are redeemed from sickness, then the devil can't put sickness on us unless we give place to him, thereby, opening the door to him.

These are three primary ways sickness enters the life of the believer, but they aren't the only ways. These aren't just ways sickness enters, but they are also three primary ways any difficulty or defeat enters.

Worry, Fear & Unbelief

The first cause the Spirit gave us that night as to how sickness, difficulty or defeat enters the life of the believer is through the loss of peace.

Mark 5:25-34

And a certain woman, which had an issue of blood twelve years, And had suffered many things of many physicians, and had spent all that she had, and was nothing bettered, but rather grew worse, When she had heard of Jesus, came in the press behind, and touched his garment. For she said, If I may touch but his clothes, I shall be whole. And straightway the fountain of her blood was dried up; and she felt in her body that she was healed of that plague. And Jesus, immediately knowing in himself that virtue had gone out of him, turned him about in the press, and said, Who touched my clothes? And his disciples said unto him, Thou seest the multitude thronging thee, and sayest thou, Who touched me? And he looked round about to see her that had done this thing. But the woman fearing and trembling, knowing what was done in her, came and fell down before him, and told him all the truth. And he said unto her, Daughter, thy faith hath made thee whole; GO IN PEACE, AND BE WHOLE of thy plague.

When this woman received healing, Jesus told her how to keep it and not lose it, *"...go in peace, and be whole...."* He let her know that if she lost her peace, she would lose her health. You have to protect your peace, for peace is imperative to your health. The Amplified Bible of Mark 5:34 reads, *"...Go in (into) peace and be CONTINUALLY healed and freed from your [distressing bodily] disease."* This carries with it the thought that as long as peace continued, healing continued. To forfeit peace would be to forfeit healing.

Peace is a fruit that God has deposited in your spirit, but it must be protected from that which would try to injure or diminish it. You don't have to try to get it. It is in your spirit, but it must be yielded to.

If there's anything that humanity longs for most, it's peace, peace in every arena of life – spiritually, mentally, and physically.

When Jesus was born, a host of angels appeared in the sky to the shepherds in the field, and their declaration was, *"...on earth PEACE good will toward men."* Jesus' arrival was announced as peace.

One of the last things Jesus told His disciples before He left the earth was, *"My peace I give into with you."* He let them know that this mighty force which governed His daily life would not exit with Him, but He was making it a present force in the lives of His children.

Peace is a mighty force that deflects the greatest of opposition. What does peace look like and act like? We can look at the earthly life of Jesus and see how it looks and acts.

Peace slept in the boat while the storm raged all around. Peace walked through the hometown crowd that tried to push Him off a cliff, and went His way through the midst of them. Peace responded to Lazarus' untimely death by staying unmoved and unhurried for four days before raising him up. Peace made every potentially explosive moment calm.

Peace doesn't fall apart in the midst of turmoil. Peace will rest while others wring their hands. Peace will rejoice while the unbelievers cry.

Years ago, I was at the home of an internationally known evangelist. His home was beautiful, but I was especially impressed by his wonderful backyard. It was beautifully landscaped and manicured. When I commented on its beauty, the evangelist stated, "Pay whatever it costs to buy peace." He was letting us know that anything that brings peace, rest and refreshing to you is worth whatever it costs.

The peace Jesus has given us is totally independent of all surrounding circumstances. His peace doesn't operate only when everything is in place and running smoothly; its greatest power is seen in the midst of turmoil. Peace doesn't mean that there's the absence of tests and trials. Peace means that in the presence of opposition, we remain unmoved by what we see and feel because we're holding to and resting on His Word.

Peace stares in the face of adversity, its gaze full of God, bringing calmness to the boisterous waves. Peace is the unflinching companion of faith. Faith in God is always accompanied by peace, otherwise, it isn't faith.

Yes, in a test the mind may be assaulted; the mind and the body may feel the effects of a test, but this only causes the peace that is in the believer's heart to rise up and still the greatest adversity.

As Isaiah wrote, *"For ye shall go out with joy, and be led forth with peace..."* (Isaiah 55:12). Peace is part of your inheritance for the journey of this life. This peace was left to you by Jesus.

Jesus' birth established peace; His daily life exuded peace; and His departure from earth bequeathed peace.

We should celebrate and delight in the words of Isaiah 53:5, *"...the chastisement of our peace was upon him...."* The punishment that purchased our peace was laid on Him. He bore that punishment so we wouldn't have to suffer.

Losing our peace opens the door to sickness, lack and anything else the enemy attacks us with.

Isaiah 26:3 tells us, *"Thou wilt keep him in PERFECT PEACE, whose mind is stayed on thee: because he trusteth in thee."* The Amplified Bible says, *"You will guard him and keep him in PERFECT AND CONSTANT PEACE whose mind...is stayed on You, because he commits himself to You, leans on You, and hopes confidently in You."*

God has provided perfect and constant peace for us, not interrupted peace. How are we going to have perfect and constant peace? This verse tells us how. *"...Whose mind is stayed on thee...."* What does it mean to have our minds stayed on Him?

Jesus is the Word made flesh. To keep our minds on God's Word is to keep our minds stayed on Him. When anything tries to violate our peace, we immediately turn our minds to what His Word says about the situation, and our peace is maintained.

Tests and trials will try to violate our peace, but we refuse their offer. Any thought that troubles us, unsettles us, puts us down, makes us feel guilty, accuses us or condemns us, is from the devil and we must resist it. The peace God gives is greater than that which would try to trouble us.

The Penalties of Worry

During the Miracle Service, when I spoke out by the Spirit the three primary ways sickness enters the life of the believer, the Spirit also said that three things will steal our peace from us if we let them.

1. Worry

To worry is to meditate in the negative direction.

Philippians 4:6 (The Amplified Bible) tells us, *"Do not fret or have any anxiety about anything...."* God tells us, *"Do not fret...",* for He knows that worry carries a penalty with it. It's not a penalty from God, but it's a penalty of disobedience. The mind is not built to conduct worry, so the mind will break down under worry. When the mind starts trying to process worry (which it can't), it starts breaking down the body also.

Remember what Jesus told the woman who was healed of the issue of blood. He told her to go in peace and be healed. If we try to go in worry, we will lose healing. Only peace can receive healing, worry can't. Worry can only receive sickness. That's why God warns us, *"Do not fret...",* for it will not only steal your peace, but it opens the door to having a troubled mind and a sick body. Worry breaks down the mind, and the devil takes advantage of a weakened mind to attack the body with sickness.

If we're not to worry, what are we to do? First Peter 5:7 (The Amplified Bible) tells us, *"Casting the whole of your care [all your anxieties, all your worries, all your concerns, once and for all] on Him, for He cares for you affectionately and cares about you watchfully."* Cast your worries on Him, and then don't touch them again in your thought life. If the temptation to worry comes back to you, say, "I've cast that worry on the Lord and I'm not taking it back. The Lord has it now – not me!"

Since God tells us, *"Do not fret..."* then that means that we have the ability to not fret. He wouldn't tell us to do something we are unable to do. But some are just in the bad habit of worry. Worry is simply a bad mental habit. It's a habit that is broken when you do as instructed in Second Corinthians 10:5, *"Casting down imaginations, and every high thing that exalteth itself against the knowledge of God, and bringing into captivity EVERY THOUGHT to the obedience of Christ."* It is a full-time job to take charge of every thought, but God is telling us that we must have a disciplined mind. We cannot have an undisciplined mind that has no restraints, thinking on anything it wants.

Have you ever been around undisciplined children? There were no restraints, boundaries or discipline exercised over them, so their behavior displayed the lack of discipline. They are unruly and full of bad habits. When parents don't discipline their children, they are setting them up to fail.

Likewise, if a believer doesn't discipline their mind, they are setting themself up to fail. The mind that is left to go any direction it wants, with no restraints, boundaries or discipline will be unruly and full of bad habits that will cause a very troubled life.

You must learn to cast down worrisome thoughts that are not in line with the Word of God. You can't cast down thoughts with thoughts. You cast down thoughts with words. You must speak to wrong thoughts, resisting them, then speak the right thought, which is the thought that's in line with the Word of God. From then on, ignore the wrong thought.

Jesus defeated Satan and spoiled principalities and powers (Colossians 2:15), stripping them of their power to harm you. But the greatest power the devil has is the power of suggestion. He suggests a thought to you to try to get you to take it. If you take it, turn it over in your mind and speak it out, then you have opened the door to him. But you must not be ignorant of Satan's devices. You must recognize the thoughts the devil may suggest, resist them, and refuse to touch them in your thought life. You can't out-think his thoughts in an attempt to get rid of them. Don't try to get rid of them, just ignore them and put your mind on something else.

If the devil can hold you in the mental arena, he'll whip you because that's his arena. He is the master of the mental arena. But learn to hold him in the arena of faith by speaking faith words out of your spirit, and then you'll whip him.

You can't believe God with your mind. The faith of God is in your spirit, not in your mind. Anytime a Christian is endeavoring to believe God but they're getting no results, it's because they're trying to believe God with their mind, not with their spirit. The mind can't conduct faith. The mind isn't equipped to believe God, but the spirit is; so don't get trapped into trying to "figure out" your answer. Your answer isn't in your mind, so don't look there; it's in your spirit, so speak out of your spirit.

I've never once walked into my kitchen and opened up the refrigerator door to look for a pair of shoes I needed. My shoes aren't kept in the refrigerator, so I don't look there for them. Likewise, faith isn't in my mind, so I don't look there for my help. I don't try to believe God with my mind. Faith is in the believer's spirit.

Worry is a tactic the enemy uses to try to hold you in the mental arena.

My husband tells of his mother who was in and out of mental institutions most of her adult life. It was worry that put her there.

When she was a young 15-year-old girl, she got pregnant. To her dad, the shame of having an unwed teenage daughter was so troubling to him that he committed suicide and left behind a suicide note stating the reason for his suicide was because of his daughter's pregnancy. That one thought tormented her for years, and drove her to alcoholism and into the mental institution.

Because she wasn't saved, she didn't know how to use the Word to cast down that tormenting thought. She ended up dying of alcoholism at 45 years of age, although she did get born again the night before she died.

Keep Fear Out

To lose our peace is to open the door to the enemy, and the Holy Spirit spotlighted three things that will steal our peace if we let them.

The first thing we listed that will rob you of your peace is worry. Now let's look at the next thing.

2. Fear

Paul writes in Second Timothy 1:7, *"For God hath not given us the spirit of fear; but of power, and of love, and of a sound mind."*

Fear is a spirit, but not a spirit from God, so it is to be resisted and not yielded to. You resist fear as you would anything that comes from the devil – by speaking to it, and telling it to leave in Jesus' Name. You can't out-think thoughts of fear; you tell them to go, and then ignore them.

God has given us the spirit of power, love and a sound mind, and these are in direct opposition to the spirit of fear. The spirit of fear opposes these and seeks to keep them from operating.

The power God has given us carries with it the authority that overcomes all opposition. Luke 10:19 records what Jesus declared to us, *"Behold, I give unto you POWER* (authority) *to tread on serpents and scorpions, and over all the power of the enemy: and nothing shall by any means hurt you."* Jesus is letting us know that when the enemy opposes us, we are to take the authority He gave us and tread on (walk right on top of) anything the enemy throws our way. And one thing He reassures us of is that when we do tread on the enemy and his works, nothing will hurt us. Don't turn and run! Rather, get on top of that situation, get on top of that spirit of fear, and forbid it to do its damage.

Not only did God give us power (authority), but He has bestowed love upon us. Love doesn't send fear to our lives. That spirit of fear is none of God's doings because God is love, and there is no fear in love. So, it never must be entertained in our thought life that fear is working as God's agent to punish or correct us because of somewhere we may have missed God. Fear is never to be permitted to linger, but is to be resisted because it is love's enemy, it's God's enemy, it's our enemy.

We've also been given a sound mind so that we can think correctly and accurately. The spirit of fear seeks to undo sound thinking so that the mind will not process thoughts soundly. Fear seeks to make someone think unreasonably, and believe the absurd to be true. If a Christian makes unsound decisions, they aren't being led by the Spirit of God because God has given us a spirit of a sound mind. If left unchecked, the spirit of fear will pervert sound thinking, but we are to forbid the spirit of fear to work its strategy against our sound minds.

I knew of one woman who was troubled by a spirit of fear. That spirit made her afraid of getting sick. She began to believe what the spirit of fear would threaten her with. She began to believe that she had critical physical conditions. Yet, when examined by the doctors, they found nothing wrong with her physically.

In ministering to her, I recognized that healing scriptures were not the remedy for her, rather she needed scriptures that taught her the authority Jesus had given her to resist the spirit of fear. I made a list of scriptures for her to meditate and act upon, but I couldn't seem to get her cooperation. She was so fully convinced of what fear told her, that the light of the Word couldn't get in. Sadly, she kept deteriorating until she died. After she died, the doctors stated, "There was never any physical reason for her to die. We didn't find anything wrong with her body." Fear had killed her. She believed what the spirit of fear told her, and when she believed it, the devil was able to work in her body what she believed.

The spirit of fear will try to bombard your mind and threaten you with all kinds of lies, but refuse to believe them. Tell Satan that he's a liar, and refuse to entertain and think upon those lies. If he can get you to believe the lies, then he'll get you speaking them. When you speak them, then he can bring them to pass; but refuse them and command them to leave.

Years ago, I heard the testimony of a minister's wife who was diagnosed with a terminal disease and was only given a few weeks to live. She started soaking herself in the Word of God and she was healed. In fact, she's still alive today (over 30 years later). But in hearing her testimony, I received insight of where she opened the door to the devil for that condition to come on her. She stated, "I don't know why that condition ever came on me. I prayed against it for ten years." That's why the sickness came on her. Fear suggested to her that she would get that sickness, and so she started praying against it. She prayed a prayer inspired by fear because she believed what the spirit of fear said to her. When she did that, she opened the door to the enemy to work that condition in her because she believed it and spoke it for over ten years.

Never let fear author your prayers. Praying words authored by the spirit of fear is still speaking fear's words. Just because they're spoken in the form of a prayer doesn't make them faith words – they're still based on fear.

If the devil suggests fearful thoughts to you, tell him that he's a liar and tell fear to go! Don't pray them! It doesn't matter whether the devil gave you a dream, a vision, or spoke audibly to you – that doesn't make them true. Tell him he's a liar, and refuse to touch those words, fears or thoughts in your thought life.

Years ago, a staff member became ill while at the office and told a secretary that they were going home early because they felt sick. The secretary later told me, "I thought to myself, 'Oh, I hope I don't get sick.' And I started rebuking sickness. But the next day I got sick. I saw then that I shouldn't have rebuked sickness, but I should have rebuked the spirit of fear." It was fear suggesting to her that she too would become sick, and she should have told that fear to go. But when she started rebuking sickness, it was because she believed what fear suggested to her. When she did that, fear won – she believed what it suggested, and she opened the door to the devil and he could then put sickness on her.

The last thing the spirit of fear wants is recognition. It wants to work undetected and unrecognized because then Christians won't properly deal with it.

Some Christians have financial problems because they're yielding to the spirit of fear regarding their finances. They think their problems are due to the lack of money, when sometimes it's because fear has entered into the way they think about and conduct their financial affairs.

Others are having financial difficulties because they have a fear of failure.

Some Christians have marriage problems because they're afraid a spouse is going to leave them.

Some people have fear dominating their homes because they're fearful that bad things are going to happen to their children.

Fear has torment with it, and that fear would like to move into every arena of your life. But you must be diligent to resist it the moment it shows up.

It comes to steal your peace, for if it can steal your peace, then it has open access to your life.

Doubt and Unbelief

There are three things that come to steal your peace. We have looked at two of them, worry and fear. Now, let's look at the last one.

3. Doubt and unbelief

The cure for doubt and unbelief is to feed your faith on the Word of God. To build your faith is to starve your doubts. Building your faith not only involves feeding on God's Word, but also involves meditating on God's Word and acting on it.

Faith is present in your spirit, not in your mind. You can't believe God with your mind. If you try to believe God with your mind, you'll slip into doubt and unbelief because the mind can't grasp what the spirit can believe. Reason is doubt in disguise. Analyzing the Word mentally will steal your faith. Don't analyze the Word, just do it!

Peace has to be in place if you're to receive from God. Worry, fear, doubt and unbelief have no ability to receive from God, but peace does.

At all costs, guard and protect the peace of God in your life from the enemies of worry, fear, doubt and unbelief. God's peace is yours, so walk in it.

Chapter 3

CAUSE #2 - TURNING FROM THE PLAN OF GOD

During the Miracle Service I mentioned in the previous chapter, the Holy Ghost gave us the three primary ways that sickness, difficulties or defeat gain entrance into the life of the believer. The first way the Spirit gave is through the loss of peace. In this chapter, we're going to look at the second way the Spirit gave – by turning the wrong direction, away from the plan of God.

When a believer turns away from God's plan, he turns away from health, supply, and all that belongs to the believer.

Long life is connected to God's plan. To veer away from God's plan is to veer away from long life. Health is in the direction of God's plan and God's Word. To step outside of God's will is to open yourself up to the attack of the enemy, and then he can attack you with sickness. It's imperative to live close to God and to stay with God's plan for your life if you're to live in divine health. If you do get out of God's will, repent and get back in as quickly as you can; then you can receive healing.

The blessings of God are conditional. You have to live in line with God's plan and God's Word for your life if you're to partake of God's best for your life. You must give your best to God if you're to receive His best.

During Jesus' earthly ministry, He let us know what sustained Him. *"…My meat is to do the will of him that sent me, and to finish His work"* (John 4:34). I like the way the Amplified Bible states this verse, *"...My food (nourishment) is to do the will (pleasure) of Him who sent Me and to accomplish and completely finish His work."*

That which fed, nourished, and sustained Jesus during His earthly ministry was to stay with God's plan for His life. The devil certainly attacked Jesus at every turn, but because Jesus stayed true to God's plan, no attack of the enemy could have its intended effect. Jesus overcame him in every opposition because He was untouchable in God's will.

The Amplified Bible of Ephesians 2:10 tells us, *"For we are...[born anew] that we may do those good works which God predestined [planned beforehand] for us [TAKING PATHS WHICH HE PREPARED AHEAD OF TIME], THAT WE SHOULD WALK IN THEM [living the good life which He pre-arranged and made ready for us to live]."* God has already laid out a plan for each one of our lives, and this verse shows us that as we live out His plan for us, that then we'll be "living the good life". The only good life is the life that lives out God's plan. To veer away or turn away from God's plan is to leave the good life. Life becomes hard when you try to live out your plan, but joy and life worth living is what His plan holds for your life.

Living God's plan for your life and walking in the light of the Word holds such great blessings and rewards, but on the other hand, to come up to light and not walk in it is dangerous. To know God's will and God's Word for your life and not walk in it is dangerous. To not seek to know God's will and plan for your life is costly.

Look at what Jesus told Saul (Paul) on the road to Damascus before his conversion.

Acts 9:3-5, Amplified Bible
Now as he (Paul) *traveled on, he came near to Damascus, and suddenly a light from heaven flashed around him, And he fell to the ground. Then he heard a*

voice saying to him, Saul, Saul, why are you persecuting me [harassing, troubling, and molesting Me]? And Saul said, Who are you, Lord? And He said, I am Jesus, Whom you are persecuting. It is DANGEROUS and it will turn out badly for you to keep kicking against the goad [to offer vain and perilous resistance].

The Role of Prayer in God's Plan

The plan God has for your life will not unfold to you all at once. He reveals it to you one step at a time, so you must continue to live close to God and keep your spirit sensitive to hear His voice so that you can live accurately, knowing each step of His plan.

As you spend time in His presence and feed on His Word, His will for your life will become clear.

As you spend time in God's presence, it's important to spend time speaking in other tongues, for First Corinthians 14:2 tells us, *"For he that speaketh in an unknown tongue speaketh not unto men, but unto God: for no man understandeth him; howbeit in the spirit he speaketh MYSTERIES."*

There are mysteries God knows about your life, and speaking in tongues is the only way you can access these mysteries.

When I need to know God's direction for my life, I take extra time to go aside and speak in other tongues. As I speak in other tongues, I quiet my mind and focus on my spirit, and as I do, clarity comes to my spirit regarding God's plan.

If you lack clarity of God's will, take time to speak in other tongues, but quiet your mind and focus on your spirit so that when you do speak in tongues, the clarity God gives to your spirit can float up and enlighten your mind; then you'll know what to do.

As we walk and live accurately in line with God's plan, we keep the door closed to the enemy, and God's best can operate in our lives.

25

Chapter 4

CAUSE #3 - LACK OF GRATITUDE

The third way the Spirit of God gave us in that Miracle Service that sickness, defeat, and the devil gain entrance into the life of the believer is through the lack of gratitude. How few Christians realize the importance of gratitude and thankfulness in the role of healing and victory.

Faith finds its greatest expression through thankfulness and gratitude toward God for all that He has done and provided for us. Praise is the voice of faith. Praising God is one way we release, express and exercise the faith that's in our hearts.

See what God warned us of in Deuteronomy 28:47 & 48 (Amplified Bible).

> *Because you did not serve the Lord your God with JOYFULNESS of [mind and] heart [in GRATITUDE] for the abundance of all [with which He had blessed you], Therefore YOU SHALL SERVE YOUR ENEMIES...*

When you fail to be joyful and thankful for God's blessings in your life, you open the door to the enemy. *"Therefore you shall serve your enemies...."* Sickness is an enemy. Lack is an enemy. Doubt is an enemy. Anything the enemy has can gain entrance into the believer's life when they cease to be joyful and grateful. The lack of gratitude is one way you can open the door to the enemy.

God's Prescription For Depression

Isaiah 61:3 instructs us, *"To appoint unto them that mourn...the oil of JOY for MOURNING, the garment of PRAISE for the SPIRIT OF HEAVINESS...."*

It's up to us to put on the "garment of praise" to get rid of depression or sadness. Praise is the cure for depression, sadness or grieving because praise is faith in action, and faith is the victory that overcometh the world, and the things in the world (First John 5:4). Praise puts God into the situation.

The Amplified Bible of Isaiah 61:3 tells us, *"To grant [consolation and joy]) to those who mourn...the oil of joy instead of mourning, the GARMENT [expressive] OF PRAISE instead of a heavy, burdened, and failing spirit...."* The reason heaviness and depression ever gain ground in the life of a believer is because they haven't been wearing their garment of praise. Regardless of circumstances or how you may feel, put praise in your mouth all throughout the day and during times of attack. By acting on the Word in this way, you release God's ability into your situation and into your life.

Behind In Praise

Many are sick today because they're behind in praise and gratitude.

When the ten lepers cried out to Jesus for healing, He instructed them to go and show themselves to the priests. As they went, they were healed. When one of the ten realized he was healed, he turned back to give thanks and gratitude to Jesus for his healing. When he fell before Jesus, He asked the man, *"...Where are the nine? There are not found that returned to give glory to God, save this stranger"* (Luke 17:16-18). Jesus was looking for them to show gratitude, but they didn't.

Those who don't show proper gratitude lack faith. Men of faith are men of gratitude and thankfulness. Praise and worship is an earmark of their faith life, for faith finds its greatest expression in praise. Faith never complains, it praises. If a man doesn't have faith enough to show gratitude, he doesn't have faith enough to receive from God.

Continual Praise

The psalmist, David, had learned the secret of "*His praise shall continually be in my mouth*," for praise holds you in health. Praise holds you in the spirit. Praise moves you from the mental arena to the spirit arena.

If praise stops, faith stops. If faith stops, God's power stops. Power flows to the measure that faith flows, and faith flows to the measure that praise and gratitude flow. Praise must be in our mouths CONTINUALLY if we are to hold ourselves in the place of healing, victory, supply and faith.

Hebrews 13:15 instructs us, *"By him therefore let us offer the sacrifice of PRAISE TO GOD CONTINUALLY, that is, the fruit of our lips giving thanks to his name."*

The Amplified Bible reads, *"Through Him, therefore, LET US CONSTANTLY AND AT ALL TIMES OFFER UP TO GOD A SACRIFICE OF PRAISE, which is the fruit of lips that THANK-FULLY ACKNOWLEDGE and confess and glorify His name."*

It is continual praise that holds us in continual victory, for continual praise holds us in a place of continually expressing faith, instead of just having moments of faith.

Praise Gets You In, Praise Gets You Out

When God's people surrounded the walls of the city of Jericho, which God said was theirs, God's final instruction to them was to shout. That shout was a voice of praise. When they did, the walls fell and they took possession of what God had given them.

When Paul and Silas had been thrown in prison stocks after having been beaten, they prayed and sang praises, and an earthquake came that broke off their stocks and flung their prison door open.

By looking at these two occasions, the walls of Jericho, and Paul and Silas in prison, we see the same truth work in both situations. Praise got God's people *into* the city, and praise got Paul and Silas *out* of jail. Sometimes there are places we need to get into, and sometimes there are places we need to get out of. Praise will get you in, and praise will get you out. There are some places you'll never get into until you praise your way in. There are some places you'll never get out of until you praise your way out. Either way, praise is the route that can get you where you need to go.

You can praise your way out of sickness and into health. You can praise your way out of need and into supply. You can praise your way out of depression and into peace.

The role of gratitude, praise and thanksgiving are all crucial to walking in victory.

Faith Never Complains

What you fail to be grateful for, you will lose. If you fail to express words of gratitude for your health, you'll lose your health. If you fail to show and speak words of gratitude for your spouse, you'll lose your spouse. (No marriage ever entered the divorce court when each spouse was speaking words of gratitude for their spouse.) If you fail to be grateful for your job, you'll lose it. If you fail to be grateful for your home, your cars, your daily supply, you'll lose them. Gratitude holds God's blessings in place in your life, and receives more. Lack of gratitude opens the door to the enemy to steal God's blessings from your life.

Murmuring, complaining and griping should never find a place in your mouth. When the Israelites murmured and griped about their journey out of Egypt, griped about the manna and water God provided, and complained against their pastor, Moses, the poisonous serpents gained entrance into their camp. Multitudes died that day because they became ungrateful for God's supply in their lives. Unbelief and doubt will complain and gripe, but faith never will!

It will never serve you well to gripe or complain about any supply God has given you – your pastor, your church, your spouse, your home, your children, your job, or your body. What you complain about, you'll lose.

We have a saying around our church and house, "The gripers get the vipers!"

We don't want to get bit by complaining or griping, because complaint is the voice of unbelief and doubt.

Praise is the language and the sound of faith. Faith has a sound, and praise is heard in that sound. Gratitude is heard in that sound.

Make your mouth do its work. Praise and gratitude to God is part of the work of those who believe. Gratitude and praise don't have a gripe or complaint in their mouth.

Praise your way into the fullness of God's supply for your life, and praise your way out of any difficulty the enemy may bring your way.

"His praise shall CONTINUALLY be in my mouth" (Psalm 34:1). Continual praise is the price of continual victory.

Chapter 5

Discerning the Lord's Body

1 Corinthians 11:29 & 30
Not discerning the Lord's body. For this cause many are weak and sickly among you, and many sleep.

When Paul wrote this letter to the church in Corinth, he was letting them know that there are causes why believers are weak, sick, and why they sleep (die prematurely). Not discerning the Lord's body is the cause that Paul lists in this verse as to why many believers, were weak, sickly and dying prematurely.

Notice that Paul stated, *"...MANY are weak and sickly among you, and MANY sleep."* Not a few, but many. There are many today in the body of Christ who would fall into this condition that Paul described in the Corinthian church.

This is the only scripture that specifically lists a cause of why Christians are weak, sickly, and dying prematurely, but in the Word many other causes are implied.

In First Corinthians 11:29 Paul lists the primary reason many Christians are failing, *"...not discerning the Lord's body."*

Two-Fold Application

There is a two-fold application this verse holds for us: discerning Jesus' physical body and His spiritual body.

The first application is to discern Jesus' physical body. Christians must discern that the cause for sin, sickness and disease was laid on Jesus. The penalty of our sin was laid on Him,

33

and He took our place in sickness. He bore away our sickness so that we would be free. When believers don't properly discern this about the Lord's body, then the devil takes advantage of them and many Christians become weak, sickly and die prematurely.

It is up to us to enforce in our lives the health that Jesus provided for us. When sickness comes, we are to discern that Jesus bore all sickness and disease for us; therefore, we forbid Satan to try to put on us what Jesus bore. *"Resist the devil, and he will flee from you"* (James 4:7). To resist sickness is to resist the devil. When Christians fail to resist sickness, they are not discerning that Jesus bore their sickness; that is a cause why they become sick. When we properly discern that Jesus bore our sickness and disease when the stripes were laid on Jesus' body, then we refuse to allow sickness to attach itself to us.

The second application of discerning the Lord's body is to discern Jesus' spiritual body, which is the Church that is in the earth today. Jesus is the Head, and the Church is His body. Since Christians are part of Jesus' body, discerning the Lord's body means we must discern how our actions will affect others in the body of Christ. When Christians don't discern how their actions will affect other believers, this is a cause of why many believers are weak, sickly and dying prematurely.

Bring Your Supply

Ephesians 4:16 says, *"...the whole body fitly joined together and compacted by that which every joint SUPPLIETH...maketh increase of the body...."* Paul is letting us know that since we are all part of the body of Christ, there is a supply for us to bring to the body. When we bring our supply to the body, then the body is increased. But the flip side of this verse would be that if we don't bring our supply, then there's not going to be increase, but decrease. We must discern how we are affecting the body of

Christ. Are we helping it to increase, or are we causing it to decrease? If we are bringing our supply to the body, then we're helping it to increase. If we're not bringing our supply, then we're causing it to decrease. It's not all about us, but it's about the whole body.

How do we bring a supply? We get planted in a local church and serve there. There are four ways we are to be a supply in a local church. We must faithfully:

1. attend services
2. give our tithes and offerings
3. pray for the pastor and the church
4. serve in the ministry of helps.

#1 - Church Attendance

We must faithfully attend church services if we are to properly honor the Lord. Luke 4:16 tells us about Jesus, *"...as his CUSTOM* (HABIT) *was, he went into the synagogue on the sabbath day...."* No one can be like Jesus without faithful church attendance because Jesus was faithful in His attendance.

The local church is the place where your spirit is educated in the Word of God. A school student must be faithful to attend school if they are to excel in academic studies. If they are unfaithful, they will fail their tests. Likewise, a Christian must be faithful to the local church for the education of their spirit. If they are unfaithful, they will not be prepared for the tests they will face, and will fail. If someone is not being spiritually educated by being faithful to their local church, they won't be able to bring the supply God intended for them to bring. They are not properly discerning how their actions are affecting the rest of the body of Christ, and they will open the door to the enemy in their life.

Church services are to be the highlight of the believer's week. Nothing else that a believer does is as important as the educating of their own spirit and getting to be with God's family. Teach your children that it is the highlight of their week to get to attend church, and teach your family to attend services with great anticipation and expectancy of what God will do.

#2 - Tithes & Offerings

When we give our tithes (10% of our increase) to our local church, and give offerings (the amount we give above the tithe), this is another way we discern the Lord's body. God's work in the earth needs to be funded, and God has ordained that it be funded through the tithes and the offerings of His people. Many have forfeited financial blessing and increase by not discerning that the tithe belongs to the Lord. When we tithe, we honor the Lord. Through our giving, we bring a supply to the local church.

#3 - Your Supply In Prayer

By praying for your pastor and the church family, there's a vital supply that you bring. Prayer plays a role in moving the plan of God forward, so you must bring your supply in prayer so that the plan of God will move forward in the local church and in the body of Christ.

A church without prayer is like a boat without power. It may drift along, but it won't go the full distance.

4 - Ministry of Helps

The local church is a family and all the congregation members are members of that local family. In a family, all its members have chores and responsibilities so that the workload is shared. The same thing is true in God's family. Every member of the local church should get involved in some capacity to share in the workload of that church. This is one way you discern the Lord's body.

Many Christians have forfeited blessings by not discerning this supply they should bring to the church family.

It's A Dangerous Thing

When we are properly discerning the Lord's body, we won't do anything that will bring harm or division to the body of Christ.

It's a dangerous thing to speak in a way that causes strife, division or offense about or among the sheep. It's a dangerous thing to speak ill of the pastor in a way that would cause sheep to lose confidence in their pastor. We must walk in love toward the body of Christ and discern how our actions and words will affect the rest of the body. Love never divides a home, a family or a congregation. Love won't do wrong to his neighbor or to the body of Christ.

Paul stated that in First Corinthians 11:29-30, *"...not discerning the Lord's body. For this cause...many sleep* (die prematurely). *"*

Chapter 6

PUT AWAY SIN

One minister made the statement after 70 years in the ministry, "We see more sick people in the church today than in the past decades because Christians today don't live consecrated, separated lives." The same minister went on to explain that there were very few terminal, devastating diseases among the congregations he had pastored years ago, but today they are more widespread through the body of Christ because of the sin in peoples lives.

Christians must judge themselves and put away sin. If they're living wrong, judge that it's wrong and put it away.

If you're going to live in divine health, you have to live close to God. Living full of the Word and full of the Spirit is the condition for God's unhindered blessings working in our lives. To live empty hinders God from working. To live in sin hinders God from working.

We forfeit God's best of healing and long life when we won't judge ourselves and put away sin. When a Christian persists in sin and wrong doing over a long period of time, they forfeit God's best in their life. God's best is that we live in divine health and fulfill the number of our days, but we must judge any sin or wrong doing in our lives, and put it away if we are to live in God's best.

First Corinthians 11:29-32 tells us, *"....not discerning the Lord's body. For this cause many are weak and sickly among you, and many sleep. For if we would judge ourselves, we should not be judged. But when we are judged, we are chastened of the Lord, that we should not be condemned with the world."* This verse tells us that if we fail to judge ourselves, then He will have to.

How does God judge someone? First Corinthians 5:5 tells us how God judges someone. *"To deliver such an one unto Satan for the destruction of the flesh, that the spirit may be saved in the day of the Lord Jesus."* Someone who persists in sin and wrongdoing is in jeopardy of turning their back on Jesus and going to hell. But if God judges them, He turns them over to Satan, who will work tragedy or sickness and disease in them, and their life will be shortened. God doesn't cause their life to be shortened, but He permits it. He permits their life to be shortened before they reach the point of turning their back on Jesus and going to hell.

In God's goodness and mercy, He intervenes by judging them and permitting their life to be shortened just so they won't go to hell. It's not God's best for someone's life to be shortened, but it sure does beat going to hell!

Revelation 2:21 & 22 records what God said, *"And I gave her SPACE TO REPENT of her fornication; and she REPENTED NOT. Behold, I will cast her into a bed, and them that commit adultery with her into great tribulation, except they repent of their deeds."*

When a Christian is persisting in sin and wrongdoing, God will give them "space to repent", but if they don't repent, they will be judged. You don't know how long that "space to repent" is, but never presume on the mercies of God and keep sinning. God is merciful to forgive us when we repent of sin, but if someone presumes He will just overlook wrongdoing while they knowingly persist in sin over a long period of time, one day they're going to run into judgment, for their "space to repent" will be gone. I've heard of some testimonies where God dealt with individuals over 30 years to judge themselves. How patient God is, but let's be quick to repent when we miss it and live under God's blessings.

Turned Over To Satan

First Corinthians 5:1-5 tells us of one incident of divine discipline during the early days of the church.

1 Corinthians 5:1-5
It is reported commonly that there is fornication among you, and such fornication as is not so much as named among the Gentiles, that one should have his father's wife. And ye are puffed up, and have not rather mourned, that he that hath done this deed might be taken away from among you. For I verily, as absent in body, but present in spirit, have judged already, as though I were present, concerning him that hath so done this deed, In the name of our Lord Jesus Christ, when ye are gathered together, and my spirit, with the power of our Lord Jesus Christ, To deliver such an one unto Satan for the destruction of the flesh, that the spirit may be saved in the day of the Lord Jesus.

In this instance, a young man had evidently taken his stepmother away from his father, and was living with her in sin, yet he was still part of the church in Corinth, and they hadn't done anything about it.

I'd like to take a side road here. Notice that because this young man was part of the church in Corinth, there was evidently a protection for him from Satan. Paul told them, *"To deliver such an one unto Satan...."* So, Satan couldn't just do anything he wanted to this man until the protection of the local church was removed from him and they delivered him over to Satan. There's protection in being in the body of Christ, in having a pastor and in being part of a local church that operates in the power of God.

41

What a sobering moment that must have been for that young man and the congregation when the pastor calls this man forward during a service and lays hands on him saying, "I deliver you over to Satan for the destruction of your flesh, that your spirit may be saved in the day of the Lord Jesus."

Now, it's to be understood that believers can't just randomly decide to turn someone over to Satan. This was to be done as the Lord directed by those in authority and when the power of the Lord was present to do so (First Corinthians 5:4).

If someone has been turned over to Satan, can it be changed? Sometimes it can, if they repent and make the needed changes. We see in Second Corinthians 2:6-10 how Paul tells the church in Corinth to forgive and comfort the man, and he is evidently restored. But it's always best to just judge ourselves to begin with, and to make any needed corrections.

Sin No More

In John 5:5-14 we read the story of the man who had an infirmity for 38 years. He was among five porches full of sick people. They were all waiting for the angel to stir the water, and the first one in the water after it was stirred was healed.

But one day, Jesus walked among the sick in that place, approached this man and told him to take up his bed and walk. Immediately the man was made whole. Later that day, Jesus found this man in the temple and gave him further instructions. *"...Behold, thou art made whole: SIN NO MORE, LEST A WORST THING COME UNTO THEE."* In this passage we see that sin opens the door to sickness. The message of divine healing is coupled with a lifestyle of holiness. We must learn to live clean and holy lives before the Lord if we're to maintain health. If we're to live healed, we must live close to God. For us to live as God desires, we must judge ourselves in the light of the Word, and make any needed corrections or adjustments.

Resisting Accusations

Now, it's to be understood that the accusations the devil tries to bring before us is not the same thing as when we judge ourselves in the light of the Word. Satan's accusations toward our minds must be resisted and cast down, or we will open the door for the enemy to put fear, guilt or depression on us.

First John 3:20 says, *"For if our HEART condemn us...."* When you've missed it and you need to judge yourself, you'll know it in your heart. But when the devil accuses us, these bombarding accusations come against the mind and they trouble us. Anything that puts you down, makes you feel guilty, depressed or shameful doesn't come from God, and it must be resisted. But if you know in your heart that you missed it, there won't be the mental torment; you'll just know in your heart that you need to judge yourself and make the needed correction.

How do you judge yourself? You just say, "I judge that as wrong. I repent of that, and I'm not going to do it anymore."

When we walk in the light of the Word, we live in great blessing. When we come up to light, let's walk in it. Let's be a doer of the Word.

Chapter 7

AN UNRENEWED MIND

The devil thrives on ignorance. He's counting on ignorance to work his plan.

Hosea 4:6 tells us, *"My people are destroyed for lack of knowledge...."* The lack of knowledge concerning what God has said in His Word is a cause of why God's people are destroyed.

Paul tells us in Romans 12:2, *"And be not conformed to this world: but BE YE TRANSFORMED BY THE RENEWING OF YOUR MIND...."* The renewed mind is the mind that takes what God says in His Word and orders his thinking and life after it.

First Peter 2:2 instructs, *"As newborn babes, desire the sincere milk of the word, that ye may GROW thereby."* Peter is telling those who are spiritual babies that if they will feed on the milk of the Word that they will grow. As they grow, they will be able to take in more than the milk of the Word, but they will then move on to enjoy the meat of the Word.

When someone is born again, they are a spiritual baby, and as they feed on the Word, they will advance from babyhood to childhood, then on to full spiritual maturity. But this process only takes place as they feed on the Word and do it as part of their daily lifestyle.

As a Christian feeds on the Word and acts on it, their mind becomes renewed. They begin to see how God thinks and how He works, and they begin to think a new way, and not the old way they used to think before they were born again.

Because this renewing of the mind is a process that takes time and effort on the part of the individual, many times it's neglected, and so some remain spiritual babies, never progressing on to full spiritual maturity. These spiritual babies not only fail to mature, but they live carnal lives. A carnal believer is someone who is ruled by their feelings, emotions and circumstances around them. The spiritual life is one who is ruled by what God has said in His Word, regardless of what their physical senses and circumstances tell them.

Defeat enters the life of the carnal Christian because they are ruled by their physical senses, and that's the arena through which the enemy gains access to their life.

A Christian is to allow the Word to govern their life, asking themself when they're faced with any difficulty, "What does the Word say?"

A carnal man is ruled by his physical senses, by what he sees and feels; but a spiritual man is one who always allows the Word to dominate him through his born again spirit. When faced with difficulties, the spiritual man draws up his answer from the Word of God that's in his spirit, for God guides the born again man through his spirit.

If one remains a spiritual baby or lives as a carnal person, sickness and disease will always have an entrance into their life. But by renewing their mind in the Word of God, and allowing the Word to govern the way they think and act, they keep the door closed to the enemy.

It takes time to get your mind renewed with the Word of God. You must take time to feed on the Word, meditate on the Word (for that's how you build it into your spirit), and act on the Word. The Word tells us that when we renew our mind with the Word of God, our life is transformed. The mind is renewed only as we act upon the Word.

Chapter 8

WALKING IN LOVE

Mark 11:25
And when ye stand praying, forgive, if ye have ought against any: that your Father also which is in heaven may forgive you your trespasses.

A way that we give place to the devil is through harboring unforgiveness toward someone. When Jesus spoke this instruction about forgiveness in Mark 11:25, it was preceded by two of the greatest scriptures on faith. *"For verily I say unto you, That whosoever shall say unto this mountain, Be thou removed, and be thou cast into the sea; and shall not doubt in his heart, but shall believe that those things which he saith shall come to pass; he shall have whatsoever he saith. Therefore I say unto you, What things soever ye desire, when ye pray, believe that ye receive them, and ye shall have them"* (Mark 11:23-24).

Although Jesus shows us what faith in God can accomplish in verses 23 and 24, He shows us in verse 25 what will keep your faith from working – unforgiveness.

Now, we know from the Word that there are other things that will keep faith from working properly, but Jesus only singled out this one thing – unforgiveness, because He knew that unforgiveness is the primary cause for faith not working.

If your faith isn't working, check here first. Make sure there's no air of unforgiveness about you.

Before you hold on to any unforgiveness, strife, bitterness, resentment, animosity, and any other like things, ask yourself, "Can I afford to be without my faith?" All these things will keep your faith from working. You know you can't afford to be in a position where your faith won't work.

Galatians 5:6 tells us, *"...faith which worketh by love."* What gasoline is to your car, love is to your faith. You can have a wonderful, expensive, beautiful car, but without gasoline, it won't go anywhere. You can have a robust, well-developed faith, but without love, it won't go anywhere. Love fuels your faith so that your faith can move in your life and bring blessings.

You can't afford to step out of love because you're going to need your faith. *"Now the just shall live by faith,"* is what the Word tells us (Hebrews 10:38). You need your faith so you can live the way God planned.

Love Keeps Sickness Out

Not walking in love will open the door to sickness in your life, and it can even open the door to sickness on your family.

One man told of how his small son developed a growth. The doctors were positive about the young boy's situation, saying that it could be easily removed through surgery, so the parents agreed to have it removed. However, shortly after the surgery, the growth came back again, but the doctors were baffled by its regrowth. A second time, the doctors removed it. Again, after a short time, the growth came back. The doctors were at a loss as to why it kept returning.

Finally, the father of the boy went to God to talk to Him about his son's physical situation. As the father was praying, the Spirit of God said to him, "Your failure to forgive your own father is the reason the enemy has gotten in to cause this condition in your son's body." The man quickly repented, seeing where he had left the door open to the devil. And when he did, the growth on his son instantly disappeared.

Now that the father was walking in forgiveness toward his own father, his faith started working and his son was healed.

Walking in love and living free from unforgiveness, resentment, offense, bitterness, and other like things, keeps the door closed to sickness.

Forgiveness Isn't A Feeling

Forgiveness is not a feeling, it's a decision. You decide to forgive someone. Even if negative feelings, thoughts and memories arise about that person, you are to say, "No, I've forgiven that person and I refuse those thoughts in Jesus' Name."

If you forgive someone, you have to forget what they did to you, too. You can't bring it up to them to try to manipulate and control them.

Isaiah 43:25 tells us that God said, *"I even I, am he that blotteth out thy transgressions for mine own sake, and WILL NOT REMEMBER thy sins."* You see, this is how God forgives. He forgives and forgets. He doesn't drag up your past sins at some opportune time to make you feel bad. So, when we forgive, we must forgive the way God forgives – He forgives and He forgets.

Forgive Yourself

Not only do you have to forgive others if you want your faith to work, but you have to forgive yourself. If you don't forgive yourself, your faith won't work.

Romans 8:1 tells us, *"There is therefore NOW NO CONDEMNATION to them which are in Christ Jesus...."* God doesn't condemn you for all the times you've missed it and sinned. You can't allow yourself to come under condemnation, meditating on all the things you've done wrong or all the times you've missed it.

If you do, you'll open the door to the devil to attack you with depression and oppression.

If the devil tries to accuse you with your past, you must exercise your faith in God's Word that says, *"If we confess our sins, he is faithful and just to forgive us our sins, and to cleanse us from all unrighteousness"* (1 John 1:9). Remind the devil that you are forgiven and cleansed, and that God has forgotten it.

How long does it take for God to forgive you and to forget it? The moment you repent you are forgiven. So, forgive yourself, forget it, and go on.

In Romans 8:1 we're told, *"There is therefore NOW NO CONDEMNATION to them which are in Christ Jesus...."* God put a timeline on the end of condemnation – NOW! It's to stop now in your life! It's to stop now in your thought life!

Keep Strife Out!

If we open the door to the enemy by failing to walk in love, it will not only affect our health, but it will also affect our finances.

Let's look at an event in the life of Abram (before his name was changed to Abraham).

Genesis 13:2, 5-9
And Abram was very rich in cattle, in silver, and in gold. And Lot also, which went with Abram, had flocks, and herds and tents. And the land was not able to bear them, that they might dwell together: for their substance was great, so that they could not dwell together. And there was a strife between the herdmen of Abram's cattle and the herdmen of Lot's cattle...And Abram said unto Lot, Let there be NO STRIFE, I pray thee, between me and thee, and between my herdmen and thy herdmen; for we be brethren. Is not the whole land before thee? separate thyself, I pray thee, from me....

At a time of wealth and increase for Abram and Lot, strife arose. Even though Abram and Lot weren't in strife with each other, their employees were, and strife can easily travel up the ranks and affect the leadership. To close the door to strife, Abram was willing to be separated from family. He knew that nothing would destroy the family like strife; nothing would destroy increase like strife.

If strife enters a family, a home, a marriage, it will cut off increase.

If there is financial difficulty in a home, one of the first things to do is make sure that strife hasn't entered in.

Before spouses get into strife, it would serve them well to ask themselves, "Do I have enough money to fund this strife?" The answer would always be that no one has enough money to fund strife, for strife will consume it.

Abram understood that even with his great wealth, he didn't have enough to fund strife.

Let's look at James 3:16. *"For where envying and strife is, there is confusion and EVERY EVIL WORK."* Envy and strife throw the door wide open to every evil work that the devil has. Envy and strife remove all restraint against the enemy's movement.

The Word tells us the solution to all conflicts, *"...walk in love, as Christ also hath loved us..."* (Ephesians 5:2). *"Love worketh no ill to his neighbor..."* (Romans 13:10).

As one minister wrote, "One step out of love is a step into sin."

If you're born again, the love of God is in you because His nature is in you, and His nature is a love nature. Romans 5:5 tells us, *"...the love of God is shed abroad in our hearts by the Holy Ghost...."* You don't have to pray that God will give you love, for it's in your spirit. As you let that love that's in you dominate you, it will grow and develop, and it will help you keep the door closed to the enemy.

Chapter 9

EXERCISING FAITH CONTINUALLY

Another cause for the enemy's entrance into the life of the believer is failure to exercise faith continually, or to fail to hold fast to what they have received.

Anything that God has provided not only has to be received, but it also must be maintained.

We know that God created the earth, the heavens and everything in them by speaking words of faith. It was faith words that brought all that is into being. But Hebrews 1:3 tells us that God *"...UPHOLDING all things by the word of His power..."* sustains all that He has created. He didn't just speak words of faith that created everything, but that faith is still moving to uphold all things.

Anything you receive from God has to be upheld and sustained, for there is an enemy arrayed against us who continually endeavors to take from us everything we have received from God.

Most Christians are familiar with the account of when Peter walked on the water, but because of becoming occupied with what he saw and heard while he was walking out that miracle, he lost the miracle and sank. Peter received a miracle, but he also lost a miracle.

Many have received answers from God for situations in their life, but because they didn't understand the importance of holding fast, they lost what they had received. First Thessalonians 5:21

instructs us to, "...*HOLD FAST that which is good.*" The instruction to hold fast lets us know that there's going to be opposition to what has been received. Some think that if God gave them something, that they will always have it; but that's not true.

God placed Adam in the Garden of Eden and gave him full authority over it, but he lost it by listening to the enemy.

Although Jesus came back and restored to the church the authority that Adam had lost, we still must hold fast and exercise our faith so we don't lose what God has blessed us with.

"*The just shall LIVE by faith.*" The exercising of faith is to be a lifestyle. We are not to have just moments of faith, but a lifestyle of faith is what's required to maintain what we receive from God.

If we're going to live a lifestyle of faith, our inward man is to be renewed day by day (Second Corinthians 4:16). We are renewed day by day as we feed on the Word, exercise our faith daily, and act on the Word.

Romans 10:17 says, "*So then faith cometh by hearing, and hearing by the word of God.*" So many Christians are trying to believe without hearing. If we quit hearing, we'll quit exercising faith.

Faith comes by hearing – by what you're hearing today. Faith doesn't come by "heard" (past tense), but by "hearing" (present tense).

First Peter 5:8-9 warns us, "*Be sober, be VIGILANT; because your adversary the devil, as a roaring lion, walketh about, seeking whom he may devour: WHOM RESIST STEADFAST* (CONTINUALLY) *IN THE FAITH....*"

We must be ever diligent to exercise our faith. We must be vigilant and watchful to keep the enemy out. To be watchful means to pay attention. Many times, things are lost out of our lives because we fail to pay attention to things in our lives. As one minister wrote, "Watchfulness is the price of constant victory."

Our exercise of faith and our confession of victory must be continual. Occasional confession produces occasional results, but continual confession produces continual results, for Mark 11:23 tells us, *"...he shall have whatsoever he saith."* The more you say it, the more you have it. The less you say it, the less you have it.

No Automatic Blessings

Even when you are in the will of God, you still must exercise faith for the supply that belongs to you to come to your life. All that God has provided for you won't just fall on you automatically, even when you're in God's perfect will; you must still exercise faith for your supply or things won't work right for you.

It is the will of God that all His people tithe to their local church and give offerings. But even as we give, we must still release our faith. The harvest won't automatically come to us; we must still exercise our faith for our harvest every time we give.

God is the One who ordained that His people should live by faith, for that's how He operates, and faith is the flow of God. As we live by faith, exercising our faith daily in our lives, we keep the door to the enemy closed, and we hold fast to God's blessings in our life.

Chapter 10

BEING LED BY THE SPIRIT OF GOD

Romans 8:14
For as many as are LED by the Spirit of God, they are the sons of God.

God will lead us by His Spirit, and if we will follow His Spirit, He will always lead us into success, but never into failure.

It's so important that we develop our human spirits to know the leading of the Spirit, but if we fail to develop our spirits to be sensitive to His leading, then we will experience difficulties we could have otherwise avoided.

God spoke to one minister saying, "If you will learn to follow My Spirit, I will make you rich. I'm not opposed to My people being rich. I'm opposed to them being covetous."

What did God mean by being "rich"? He wasn't saying that He would make all of His children millionaires. "Rich" means a full supply. God wants all of His children to have a full supply, for then they will have all their needs met and have enough to be able to give to others.

But the condition God gave when He spoke to the minister was, "IF you will learn to follow My Spirit...." If you develop your own human spirit, then your spirit will be sensitive to recognize the voice of the Holy Spirit. But, if you don't develop your own spirit, then it will be dull and won't perceive the leading of the Spirit.

How do we develop our spirit?

1. Feed and meditate on the Word
2. Act on the Word
3. Fellowship with God
4. Speak in other tongues

God has given us these means whereby we can develop our spirit, but the responsibility to develop our spirit rests with us and not with God.

If we will develop our human spirit, then we will be keen and perceive the leadings of the Lord, and we will experience success in all the affairs of life.

It costs us much to make missed steps. It costs us time, money and much difficulty. The time we spend to develop our spirit is well worth it, for it saves us from much hardship and difficulties.

Sensitive in Prayer

Not only must we learn to be sensitive to the Spirit in our everyday lives, but we must be sensitive to the Holy Spirit in prayer.

If we will make our spirit sensitive to the Holy Spirit by feeding and acting on the Word, and by praying in other tongues, we will perceive the leadings of the Spirit more accurately.

If we will be sensitive to the Holy Spirit in prayer, He will help us to pray in ways that will change situations that need changing.

He will also help us to change and abort some things the enemy wants to do in our life and in the lives of others. But if we don't develop our spirit to be sensitive to the Holy Spirit, we will miss the leadings of the Spirit. Sometimes tragedy and difficult things occur that could have been avoided if we would have been sensitive to the Spirit.

If we fail to develop our spirit, it becomes a way we give place to the enemy. But if we will faithfully develop our spirits, we give place to the Spirit of God and the success He leads us into.

Chapter 11

THE NEED FOR A PASTOR

Matthew 9:36
But when he (Jesus) *saw the multitudes, he was moved with compassion on them, because they fainted, and were scattered abroad, as sheep having no shepherd.*

Many Christians open the door to the enemy to attack them by failing to have a pastor, or by leaving the pastor God assigned to their life.

Jesus noted the condition of those sheep who had no shepherd – they were sick, they were fainting, and they were scattered.

God has given pastors as one of the fivefold gifts to the body of Christ. The most needful and important fivefold office in the life of the sheep is that of a pastor.

If a Christian has a pastor, they are offered protection from fainting or being scattered. If a Christian faints, they won't finish their race. Yes, they will still go to heaven, but they won't complete their assignment on the earth; they will fall short of finishing their race. If a Christian is scattered, then every arena of his life will show the effects of that. Their marriage, children, health, finances and purpose will be scattered out of their place.

To have a pastor means more than just attending a church. It means to receive your pastor as a divine supply into your life, and honoring that office in your life. To have a pastor means that you receive his Word-based sermons as God's instruction for your life, and you hear the Word preached with the purpose of being a doer of the Word.

It's life and death what church you attend. It's important that the church you attend holds to teaching the truths of God's Word because every arena of your life is going to need God's Word in order for you to live in the success God has planned for you.

If you attend a church that doesn't believe in healing, you won't get healed there. If you attend a church that doesn't believe in prosperity, lack will move into your life. It's life and death what church you go to!

Every Christian should allow the Lord to lead them in choosing a church to attend, for God will lead you to a place where you will be spiritually nourished.

Stay Where God Puts You

When God directs you to a church to attend, then stay there. Don't leave unless God tells you to leave. Many Christians open the door to the devil by jumping from church to church. God isn't fickle. He won't lead you to jump from church to church. He wants you to plant yourself in the church He leads you to.

When God leads you to a local church, it's because He intends to bring the supply to your life through that pastor and through that local body of believers. You can't attend just any church and receive the supply God intends for you to have. God will supply your life through the pastor He leads you to. So, don't let any offense or difficulty run you out of the place God leads you to.

I know which ministers God has put in my life to be a supply to me, for every time I hear them minister, God speaks to me and I receive revelation.

I can't just sit under any minister and receive my supply. I have to stay under those that God has assigned to feed my life.

When you're under the pastor God has assigned to your life, you'll be fed. God will speak to you when you're under the pastor He has for you.

Go where you're fed!

One of the primary devices the enemy uses against God's people is to try to pull them away from their pastor, who is a divine supply in their life. If he can pull them away, then he can cause them to faint and he will scatter their life.

The devices the enemy uses are strife, offense, unforgiveness, and other like things to pull you away from your pastor; but if you leave the place of divine supply under your pastor without God telling you to leave, you open the door to the devil, and he can gain access into your life and your family.

The pastoral anointing provides safety for your life. Don't let anything rob you of that safety.

Stay in the church God leads you to, and don't leave unless God releases you because God intends to bless and increase you there.

Chapter 12

KEEP PACE WITH GOD'S PLAN

After Jesus was raised from the dead, He appeared to His disciples to give them further instruction. *"But ye shall receive power, after that the Holy Ghost is come upon you: and ye shall be witnesses unto me both in Jerusalem, and in all Judaea, and in Samaria, and unto the uttermost part of the earth"* (Acts 1:8). From this scripture we can see that when they were filled with the Holy Ghost while in Jerusalem, they were to carry that power beyond Jerusalem and into Judaea, Samaria, then to the uttermost part of the earth.

In Acts 7 & 8 we see the church come under great persecution. In Acts 7 we see the stoning of Stephen, and after that we see persecution break out against the church. Acts 8:1 reads, *"...And at that time there was a great persecution against the church which was at JERUSALEM; and they were all scattered abroad throughout the regions of JUDAEA and SAMARIA...."* Acts 8:4 goes on to tell us, *"Therefore they that were scattered abroad went EVERY WHERE preaching the word."* When the persecution breaks out against the church in Jerusalem, they are scattered to Judaea and Samaria, then everywhere. That's the instruction Jesus gave them years before right before the Day of Pentecost, the day the Holy Spirit was poured out on the earth. Jesus told them that they were to carry this power beyond Jerusalem, into Judaea, Samaria, and to the uttermost part of the earth.

When the persecution broke out against the church, it forced them to carry the Gospel beyond Jerusalem into Judaea, Samaria and everywhere else. If they had obeyed what Jesus told them in the beginning, the persecution would never have broken out against them. Although God wasn't the One who sent the persecution, God allowed the persecution so that they would scatter out of Jerusalem and carry the Gospel everywhere. It wasn't God's best that they face this persecution, but because they were moving too slowly and weren't keeping pace with God's plan, they opened the door to the devil.

It was after this persecution arose, scattering the church out of Jerusalem, that Philip went down to Samaria and had a mighty revival that we read about in Acts 8. God wanted the Gospel to be spread everywhere, but the church got in a rut and stayed where they had been, there in Jerusalem.

Don't Get In A Rut

How easy it is to stay where you've been. If we're not careful, we'll get rutted in a certain place and not move forward into what God has for us, and then we fail to keep pace with God's plan. When we do that, difficulties and persecution can arise that could have been avoided if we hadn't gotten into a rut.

Now, don't misunderstand me. Some people don't take time to hear from God and they just jump from one thing to the next, never really producing any fruit anywhere. I'm not referring to that. But we must be careful that we don't assume that we'll stay where we've always been, and fail to be ready to move with God whenever He says to move.

I heard one pastor, who had been a missionary years before, say, "I always keep one bag packed, because I want God to know that I'm ready to go if He says to go." This pastor showed that he had a pilgrim spirit; he had a spirit of faith. Even though this man pastored the same church in the same city for over 30 years, he kept his spirit alert and ready to move at a moment's notice – that's faith! Doubt and unbelief want to settle down into one place and one position with nothing to unsettle or disturb it, but faith is ever ready to make a move when God directs. Don't assume you'll always stay where you've always been.

Even if God puts you in one location and keeps you there for the rest of your life, you still have to be inwardly ready to go at a moment's notice. You must still inwardly reach out for more, even though you may stay in the same location for a lifetime. The faith in you won't leave you in a stationary position, even if you do stay in one location for your entire life.

Abraham had a pilgrim spirit. He was ever looking to God to guide him to the next place He had for him. That's faith. Faith doesn't mean that you're always physically on the move, but faith means that you're reaching forward to bring more of God to the location where God puts you. Faith will stretch you. Faith won't let you settle down in a stationary position without reaching for more.

Paul said in Philippians 3:14, *"I PRESS toward the mark for the prize of the high calling of God in Christ Jesus."* Even if God puts you in one location that you never move from, you must still press to have more of God in that location. If you stop pressing, you'll get rutted in that place and not be as effective as you should be. Not only that, if you get rutted, you will likely miss the direction of God if He tries to lead you to a different place. This is a real danger with those in the fivefold ministry, as well as with any believer. If we're not careful, we'll quickly become settled down into a location, a position, or even a fivefold office, and not allow anything to budge us.

This is one of the things that impresses me so much about my husband. He is quick to perceive and understand the transitions that God leads him into. He is quick to recognize when God is changing a season in his life. He's quick to properly indentify it, and to move with it. I can't ever remember seeing my husband get into a rut of any kind! And he's worked hard to keep those around him out of ruts.

Faith has a press to it, and faith refuses to find any comfort in a rut.

My husband pastored a church for 8 years in Torrance, California, during the 1970's and early 1980's. But one day he walked into the church and he perceived in his spirit that he was done there. He knew that he had taken that congregation as far as he could take them. Then God said, "Move to Tulsa, Oklahoma." Immediately he announced it to his congregation and began moving that direction. He moved the congregation into a smaller building, because he knew that the faith of the congregation could better support a smaller building than the larger building.

A lot of pastors would have assumed that because they had been pastoring for so many years, that they would always continue to pastor. But you have to be open to the leading of God and not get rutted into an office. Many times God will allow someone to function in a particular office so that He can train and prepare them for a higher office they are intended to occupy. If that's the case, you have to move with God and change when the seasons of your life change.

After Ed moved to Tulsa, we met and married there, then we built and started a church in a town outside of Tulsa. We were in that church for about three years when Ed walked into the church building one Sunday morning, turned to me and said, "I'm done here. When I walked in the building this morning, I knew I was done. God has told me to go back to California and get in position for this next era." Then he immediately got up and announced it to the congregation that same Sunday.

Because we had the church building and 85 acres of property there in Tulsa, Ed wanted to sell it before we made the move to

California. But as we waited for the next year and a half for the building to sell, our finances started drying up, and Ed's road meetings started drying up. Ed went to God and asked, "Why are the finances and the invitations to minister on the road drying up?"

God answered, "I told you a year and a half ago to move back to California." Ed got it! He was waiting for natural things to move into place before we relocated to California. He was waiting for the sale of the church property, but when God says move, we can't let natural things decide when we obey. As we obey the word God speaks, then the natural things will fall into place.

So, I left for California on one day and had rented a home the next day. But because we had been slow to move after God had directed us, we suffered financially. Things were tight for a couple of years. God helped us and we eventually came out of it, but if we had made the transition when God said to, we would have avoided that financial hardship.

When we face difficulties like that, there's always a cause. The cause of why a lot of ministers and believers face tests and difficulties that could have been avoided is because they don't keep pace with the plan of God. They didn't make a turn when God told them to make a turn. They didn't make a change after God had told them to make a change.

You know that if you get behind financially, you can also get caught up. Likewise, if you get behind in the plan of God, you can get caught up. It's best to just keep pace with the plan of God. How do you do that? Feed on God's Word, and spend much time praying in the Holy Spirit until God's direction becomes clear in your spirit. Many times people are waiting to hear a voice speak to them before they will move, but we don't seek to hear a voice. It's clarity in our spirit we need. We must take time to get things clear in our spirit, then move with that.

By moving too slowly or moving too fast, we can face difficulties and hardships that could have been avoided. That's what happened to the church in Jerusalem. They were too slow to move on the direction Jesus gave them in Acts 1:8, and it cost them much.

When you sense a change in your spirit, take time to pray in other tongues until you gain clarity, then move forward with God and move forward into blessing.

Chapter 13

WRONG FELLOWSHIP AND COMPANIONS

1 Corinthians 15:33, Amplified Bible
Do not be so deceived and misled! Evil companionships (communion, associations) corrupt and deprave good manners and morals and character.

This scripture lets us know another way we can open the door to the enemy in our lives, and that is through having wrong fellowship and wrong companions in our lives.

We are to always bring a good testimony and be a good example to the lives of people we come into contact with, but we are not to allow personal, close fellowship with just anyone. We are to love all people, but we aren't to allow all people to have access to our lives, allowing them to speak into our lives.

When God wants to bless your life, he sends a person. When the devil wants to harm and injure your life, he sends a person. One of the things that every Christian must do is closely guard their life and their family from wrong fellowship.

As a parent, your greatest job will be two-fold:

1. Raise and keep your children in a local church
2. Closely guard who you let them fellowship with

Pay attention to who your kids are in fellowship with. If you will faithfully do these two things, you will save yourself much difficulty and heartbreak.

In allowing fellowship for our two sons, it was not enough that a friend of theirs be a Christian; but their friends had to be those who were having their minds renewed with the Word of God.

A person can get saved, but if they don't get their mind renewed with the Word of God, their life can look just like the life of someone unsaved.

For adults, the criteria for fellowship is the same. Don't allow close fellowship into your life with people who aren't growing in their spiritual lives.

Now, you may have unsaved family members who surround your life. I'm not saying to cut them off from your life, but you need to understand that you can't let people speak into your life and take counsel from those who have no knowledge of God or His Word. You can be friendly, loving and hospitable without looking to them to speak guidance into your life.

The best spiritual fellowship you'll find for your life is with those who are moving forward with God, and with those from your church family. That's the place where you should find those who are of like faith.

Wrong Fellowship Brings Wrong Things

If you open your life up to wrong fellowship, wrong things will begin happening to you.

Let's look at a well-known Old Testament event to see this. God spoke to Jonah, the prophet, telling him to go preach to the city of Ninevah. But Jonah didn't want to do that, so instead he went to Joppa and bought a ticket on a boat that was sailing to Tarshish. (Anytime you choose to go in a different direction than God sends you, you're going to have to pay for the ticket yourself, God won't!)

While at sea, a storm arose, and the men on board began to call on their gods for deliverance, but no deliverance came.

Finally, Jonah, knowing that he was disobeying the Word of the Lord, confessed to the men on board that his disobedience was the cause for the storm, and if they would throw him overboard, the storm would stop and their lives would be spared.

But the men made every other effort they could to survive without having to throw Jonah over. Finally, they realized that their desperate attempts to save the ship were useless. So, they finally consented with Jonah and threw him overboard.

You will well remember the story of how God sent a whale that delivered Jonah to dry land, and he did obey God by going and preaching to the city of Ninevah.

What I wanted you to see from this story is how the lives of the other men on board the ship were endangered because of Jonah. Those men weren't the ones who were running from God, but when they got around Jonah, wrong things started happening to them because of him.

If you allow wrong fellowship into your life or into the lives of your children, wrong things will start happening in your life and in your family.

Protect yourself and your family from unnecessary difficulties and hardships by closely guarding who is allowed to enter your life.

Fellowship Gone Wrong

We've seen people lose their businesses and homes from closely fellowshipping with and taking wrong counsel from people who didn't live or speak in line with God's Word.

God put a divine partnership together when He sent Paul and Barnabas together on missionary journeys (Acts 13:2), but in the course of their ministry, Barnabas determined to have his own way (Acts 15:37), and when he did, Paul had to let him go his way.

God may send someone into your life, but if they turn and go the wrong way, you have to let them go. Don't hold to fellowship gone wrong, no matter how long you've known them.

Stay in fellowship with those who are going forward in God, and your life and family will see the rewards of right, godly fellowship.

Chapter 14

WRONG PLACES

Another way Christians can give place to the devil is by going to wrong places. You can't return out of curiosity to places God has delivered you from.

Proverbs 5:8, the Amplified Bible, warns us, *"Let your way in life be far from her* (the loose woman)*, and come not near the door of her house [AVOID THE VERY SCENES OF TEMPTA-TION]."*

When God has brought you out of wrong fellowships, don't give them a call to see how they're doing. That is a device the enemy will often suggest, but if God lays them on your heart, you can pray for them from a distance without having to revisit those wrong places.

Wrong places hold wrong things and wrong people. You can't flirt with that which is wrong and expect the outcome to be blessed. Protect the blessing of God on your life by avoiding wrong places.

Chapter 15

LISTEN UP!

One way believers can give place to the devil is by not listening – not listening to God, not listening to the Word, not listening to their pastor, not listening to their spouse or not listening to godly counsel.

Let's look at Hebrews 11:7, The Amplified Bible. *"[Prompted] by faith Noah, being forewarned by God concerning events of which as yet there was no visible sign, TOOK HEED* (HE LISTENED) *and diligently and reverently constructed and prepared an ark for the deliverance of his own family."*

Because Noah listened to God, he and his whole family were delivered while every other family was destroyed.

Noah is listed as one of the heroes in this great list of men of faith in Hebrews 11, so we know this – men of faith are men who listen.

When someone won't listen or doesn't have any regard for the counsel of those who know God, they lack faith.

Let's look again at Hebrews 11:7, *"[Prompted] by FAITH...."* It doesn't say that Noah was prompted by God, although we know God spoke to him. It doesn't say that Noah was prompted by the Spirit of God. What prompted him to act on what God said? FAITH! He acted on what God said because he had faith!

When Christians don't act on what God says to them, it's because they lack faith – it's a faith issue. When Christians don't act on godly counsel they're given, it's because they lack faith – it's a faith issue.

Men of faith will listen and act – they will listen to God, and they will listen to those who know God, and they'll act on what they hear.

For 100 years Noah preached of the coming judgment, but no one listened. It cost them their lives, for the flood came as Noah had warned. But when the flood started coming, their opportunity to listen was past.

Much can be lost when we don't listen.

"Most People Don't Listen"

We were around one man of God during the latter months of his life who we have great regard for. Around the dinner table, he told of the different times God had sent him to warn fellow ministers about changes they needed to make in their lives if they were to live out the full length of their lives. But even after warning them, they didn't make the changes. Then the minister stated, "Most people don't listen."

When somebody knows God and their life bears the fruit of having walked with God, we would benefit by listening to them. Yes, it is to be understood that we must always ultimately follow what the Spirit of God says to our own spirit, but the Spirit will, many times, confirm what He's saying to us through someone who knows God, so we need to listen up!

Loss Of Wealth

In Acts 27 we see the account of when Paul was placed as a prisoner aboard a ship to Rome. Before they set sail, Paul warned them not to set sail, for he perceived that there would be much loss, even putting their lives in jeopardy, but they didn't listen. The coming days played out just as Paul had warned. They encountered a storm that caused them to despair of life. In desperation, they threw all their cargo overboard in an attempt to save themselves.

After an angel appeared to Paul and let him know that all who stayed with the ship would have their lives spared, the crew listened to him this time. However, if they would have listened to him earlier, they wouldn't have lost all the wealth of the cargo they had thrown overboard and they wouldn't have lost the ship.

Many face financial difficulty or financial ruin because they don't listen. God wants to protect us from loss, but we have to listen to Him before He can help us.

Who Are You Listening To?

Some don't know who to listen to. They end up listening to someone who has bad fruit in their life. But if you're going to succeed in life, you need to identify who is right to listen to.

Listen to those who are bearing good fruit in their life. Jesus told us that we would know someone by their fruit.

I love a story that I heard about a world-renowned evangelist. This evangelist was meeting with an apostle for lunch. The apostle and his office administrator arrived first at the restaurant, so they were already seated at the table when the evangelist arrived. The evangelist brought along with him his financial man. All four men stood as they greeted each other and exchanged introductions. Although the evangelist and apostle had known each other for decades, they had never met the companions each of them brought.

After concluding their introductions, all four of the men sat down.

The apostle, who was seated directly across from the evangelist, stared straight at the evangelist and said while he pointed to the financial man seated next to the evangelist, "Don't you know that this man isn't right and he's going to hurt you?"

Without any hesitation or further questioning, the evangelist turned to his financial man and said, "You're fired!"

This evangelist was a man of faith. How do we know? Faith will listen and obey when it knows that God has spoken. That apostle was warning the evangelist by the Spirit of God that his financial man wasn't safe, and he listened to him. He didn't argue, he didn't make a rebuttal, he didn't ask questions, he didn't ask the apostle for a private counseling time – he acted.

When people listen, they act. If they don't act on the instruction, they didn't listen, no matter how much they verbally agreed with what they heard. I've had many to verbally agree and acknowledge that counsel I gave them was right, but then they went out and did the exact opposite thing. They didn't listen!

If you argue with or "talk over" people who are giving you your answer, you'll never hear. If you argue, you didn't listen. If you make a rebuttal, you dismissed your answer.

When you come to church, come to hear. Come to listen to what the Word says because it holds your answer. It's not what you're doing right that's hurting your life – it's what you're doing wrong. So, come to hear the Word with the purpose of making any needed corrections to your life. How positive that is. How safe that is. The Word tells us that we are changed from glory to glory. More glory comes when we make changes, so let's hear and listen for any changes we need to make.

Your faith will never surpass your listening. The better you listen, the greater your faith, then the greater your success.

So, listen up – your success depends upon it!

Chapter 16

HONORING YOUR SPOUSE

Another way you can open the door to the enemy is by not honoring your spouse. First Peter 3:7 instructs husbands to, *"...dwell with them* (their wife) *according to knowledge, giving honour unto the wife, as unto the weaker vessel, and as being heirs together of the grace of life; THAT YOUR PRAYERS BE NOT HINDERED."*

Peter tells us that when the husband doesn't treat his wife honorably, his prayers are hindered. A prayer that's hindered is a prayer that goes unanswered.

Now, if God expects the husband to treat his wife honorably, don't you think that God would expect the wife to treat her husband honorably too? Of course He does.

Paul wrote to the church at Ephesus and instructed the men to love their wives as themselves (Ephesians 5:33). Paul also told the wives in the same verse that they are to reverence their husbands.

Look at how the Amplified Bible reads in Ephesians 5:33. *"...Let the wife see that she respects and reverences her husband [that she notices him, regards him, honors him, prefers him, venerates, and esteems him; and that she defers to him, praises him, and loves and admires him exceedingly]."*

If you honor your spouse as instructed in the Word, the rewards in your marriage and home will be great. But failure to honor your spouse will devastate the marriage and home. It will open the door to failure in every arena of your life: spiritually, mentally, physically, financially and with your children.

Many couples don't understand that much difficulty they have with their children may be due to the way they treat their spouse. If you sow dishonor toward your spouse, you can reap dishonor from your children.

Your fellowship with God, your health, your finances, and your children are all affected by how spouses treat each other in their marriage.

There are those who have even had their lives shortened because they habitually treated their spouses dishonorably.

The royal law of love is to find its highest flow in our homes and in our marriages.

God intended that we live days of heaven on earth, and that can only be accomplished as we walk in the light of God's Word. Regarding our marriages, the Word is to govern us, and as it does, we keep the door to the enemy closed.

Chapter 17

MISPLACED PRIORITIES

We must follow the guidelines God laid out for us in His Word. God shows us in His Word what is to be priority in our life. But, if we have misplaced priorities, we can open the door to the enemy.

Matthew 6:33 tells us, *"But seek ye FIRST the kingdom of God, and his righteousness; and all these things* (the provision for your daily life) *shall be added unto you."*

This verse shows us what is to be priority; we are to seek first the kingdom of God.

The kingdom of God is not a financial kingdom, it's not a business kingdom, it's a spiritual kingdom. We are to put spiritual things first.

If we fail to put spiritual things first, then our priorities get out of place, and we open the door to the devil.

Matthew 6:33 tells us, *"But seek ye FIRST the kingdom of God...."* It doesn't say, "Seek ye ONLY the kingdom of God." God knows that there are many responsibilities in our life, and He doesn't want us to neglect those responsibilities and other interests. He is telling us that our spiritual life must come first. Spiritual matters are to take the lead in our life.

If Christians get their priorities misplaced, they start putting work, children, and recreation first. When that happens, they will start encountering difficulties that could have been avoided.

Before you take that job promotion that may mean more money, consider first how it will affect your spiritual life. Will it keep you from attending church services? Will it intrude into your ability to serve in the ministry of helps in your local church? Will it cause you to have to move to a location that doesn't even have a Word church? Will it affect your family's ability to attend and serve in your church?

All these things must be considered if your spiritual life is going to hold its proper priority.

Is God First In Your Finances?

What about your finances? Do spiritual things have first place when it comes to your finances? Are you giving the tithe (tithe means 10%) of all your increase to your local church? If God is first in your finances, you will be tithing faithfully to your local church.

We have a saying in our home and in our church. "If the church needs new carpet and our home needs new carpet, guess who gets the carpet! The church!" God comes first in our finances.

We know that when we put God first in our finances, that we will never lack, but we will always be fully supplied.

Protect Your Children From Failure

What about putting God first in raising your children? Do you teach your kids that the local church is more important than the sports team? It's fine and good to have children involved in sports and other activities, but you must always teach them that church comes first.

When our boys were growing up, we always taught them that they weren't going to miss church services and church events so they could participate in sports or other activities. We taught our children that God came first. On occasion there may be a conflict between church and another activity where church was missed, but that was the exception and not the rule.

Many Christian parents have problems with their older kids today because they never properly taught their kids that spiritual things and their church was to have priority over other events and activities.

We teach our children and our congregation that church services are the highlight of their week. Nothing else they do during the week is as important as the church services, because we're teaching them that this is a way that they keep God first in their lives.

No other responsibility they have or event they are a part of is teaching them about God. Other things may be important, but they are not as important as their spiritual life. The church services are the only weekly events that are feeding and developing their spiritual lives.

The Word instructs us that we are to train up a child in the way he should go, not the way he wants to go (Proverbs 22:6). We should train them that their spiritual life and the local church come first, and then they'll go that way. To not train our children right is to open them up to failure.

The enemy likes it when Christians get their priorities misplaced because then he can get an advantage over them. But if we will be doers of the Word by putting spiritual things first in our lives, we hold the enemy in his place of defeat.

Chapter 18

FAITHFULNESS

Proverbs 28:20 says, *"A faithful man shall abound with blessings...."* A faithful man is a consistent man. But the flip side of that verse would read, "An unfaithful man shall not abound with blessings." An unfaithful man is an inconsistent man.

Blessings won't abound with the man who just has moments of faithfulness. No, he must have a lifestyle of faithfulness.

If someone is unfaithful, he opens the door to the enemy in his life.

If a man is faithful, he will be faithful in every arena of life, not just in a few arenas.

If we are going to walk in God's best, we must be faithful (consistent) in:

- our fellowship with God
- the doing of the Word
- the exercising of faith
- our church attendance
- our tithes and offerings
- our serving in the local church
- our marriage
- our employment

We want to hear Jesus say to us, "Well done, thou good and faithful servant." But that means that we must be faithful if we're to hear it. If we want to receive God's best, we must give our best.

Chapter 19

THE ORDER OF THE SPIRIT

1 Corinthians 14:4
He that speaketh in an unknown tongue edifieth himself...

When we take time to speak in other tongues, we cooperate with the Holy Spirit and with the plan that God has for our life. It is God's plan that His children be edified.

The Amplified Bible of First Corinthians 14:4 reads, *"He who speaks in a [strange] tongue edifies and IMPROVES HIM-SELF...."* It is God's plan that the believer build up and improve himself spiritually, and He has provided the means whereby that can be done – through speaking in other tongues.

One definition of the word "edify" is "to organize". So, we could properly read First Corinthians 14:4 as, "He that speaks in an unknown tongue ORGANIZES himself."

God is a God of order. Because of God's mastery of order, the solar system has perfect order. God knew that it was not enough to create all that is, but that it needed to be upheld. Hebrews 1:3 tells us that He is, *"...UPHOLDING all things by the word of his power...."* The Amplified Bible reads that God is, *"...upholding and maintaining and guiding and propelling the universe by His mighty word of power...."* This lets us know that by the Word of God's power, God is upholding and keeping the order of what He created. The universe continues to function because of this proper order.

Proper Order Brings Multiplication

Multitudes had been with Jesus for days as they listened to His teachings, but He wanted to feed them before they journeyed back to their homes, so the disciples brought Him the loaves and fishes from a little boy's lunch. The next thing Jesus did was to instruct the disciples to have the multitudes sit down in companies of fifty (Luke 9:14).

After the disciples had organized the multitudes, then Jesus prayed over the food, had the disciples to distribute it, and it was multiplied.

Notice that the multiplication came after there was proper order.

Many believers don't experience the kind of multiplication God wants for them because they are unorganized. If God sent multiplication into a setting of disorder, there would be multiplied disorder.

It is important to receiving increase that there be proper order in the life of the believer: spiritually, mentally, physically, and materially.

We are not left to implement and maintain proper order in every arena just by mere human effort, but we have divine assistance to help us implement and maintain proper order in our lives. *"He that speaketh in an unknown tongue edifieth* (organizes) *himself."* By speaking in other tongues, we cooperate with the Holy Spirit to help us build the order of God in our lives.

An Order That Caters To The Spirit

It's to be understood that there is an order that hinders the Spirit of God. When the mind of man reasons and calculates apart from the Word of God and the Spirit of God, we hinder God's movement in our lives. But there is an order that caters to the Spirit of God in our lives. This is an order that flows from the spirit of man as he walks in the light of the Word and is led by the Spirit of God. By praying much in other tongues, a believer accesses divine help in living in an order that caters to God, and doesn't hinder or limit Him.

We must have divine order in every arena of our lives: spiritually, mentally, physically and materially.

To give an example that shows the importance of order, I am reminded of a story one minister told. There was a ministry that had a nationwide weekly television broadcast that was funded by the viewers. For years they had always had the funds needed to pay for their weekly broadcast, but suddenly the financial support dropped dramatically. The pastor began praying about the situation. As his administrator walked through the ministry offices, the Spirit of God spoke and directed her to go into one of the ministry storage rooms. As she walked into the storage room, she saw television equipment stacked in total disarray all over the room. When she saw this, the Spirit of God spoke again and said, "Until the equipment that you already have is properly organized, the supply for more won't be coming."

Proper order and organization is imperative if there's going to be increase in our lives, but we're not left alone to accomplish this – we have a divine Helper, the Holy Spirit.

As we take time to speak in other tongues, God will enlighten us by His Spirit as to that which needs to be put in order in our lives, and He will empower us to make any changes. So, take time to speak in other tongues and employ God's divine help.

Chapter 20

HEARING AND DOING

James 1:22
But be ye DOERS of the word, and not hearers only....

Matthew 7:24 & 26
Therefore whosoever heareth these sayings of mine, and DOETH them, I will liken him unto a wise man....

And every one that heareth these sayings of mine, and doeth them not, shall be likened unto a foolish man....

From these scriptures we can see that it's those who hear and do the Word that are blessed. Just hearing the Word won't make a difference in your life until you do it. Faith acts on the Word. You're not in faith until you act on the Word. Just knowing what the Word says isn't enough. It's when you act on the Word in your everyday life that the victory is secured.

It's dangerous to come up to light and not walk in it. The light is the revelation of the Word that dawns on your spirit. To walk in the light means to walk in the revelation of God's Word that you receive.

So many Christians get concerned about what they don't know, but they just need to walk in the light of what they do know, and then more light will come. Many open the door to the enemy by failing to do the Word they know.

James 4:17 tells us, *"Therefore to him that knoweth to do good, and doeth it not, to him it is sin."* James tells us that if we don't walk in the light that we have, it's a sin.

When we know not to worry, but we still do it, it's sin.

God has taught us so much out of His Word, and we move into blessings when we walk in the light of the Word that we know.

What about some specific things concerning our own lives that God has spoken to our spirits about doing? If we fail to do those things He has spoken to us about specifically, we're not being a doer of the Word, and when we don't do what we know, it turns out badly for us.

It's the doer of the Word that's blessed, so let's keep the door to the enemy closed by being a doer of God's Word.

Chapter 21

NEGLIGENCE

Being negligent toward the things of God's Word will cost us much. Being negligent toward the things He has specifically told us to do can cause us hardship.

Because Jesus has spoiled principalities and powers (Colossians 2:15), Satan cannot defeat us, but negligence toward God's Word can destroy us.

Some are negligent to find out what God's Word tells us belongs to us. God warned us in Hosea 4:6, *"My people are destroyed for lack of knowledge...."* The devil needs ignorance to work his plan; he counts on people's ignorance so he can work unhindered. But if we'll take time to know God's Word for ourselves, and become doers of that Word, then we'll hold the enemy in his place of defeat.

Faith Must Be Released

Even though God has given to every believer the measure of faith (Romans 12:3), we must not neglect to feed and exercise that faith.

God gave us all the same measure of faith when we were born again. God didn't give one person a greater measure of faith than He gave another. He gave us all the same measure of faith. But from there, it is up to us to cause our measure of faith to grow, and to exercise the faith we do have.

What is it that causes your faith to grow? Romans 10:17 tells us, *"So then faith cometh by hearing, and hearing by the word of God."* As we feed on God's Word, faith comes. The Word is faith food; it's food for our spirits. You don't get faith by praying for it. Faith comes as you feed on God's Word. You don't have to try to get faith. Just feed your spirit on God's Word and faith will be there.

Now, faith comes by hearing the Word of God, but faith doesn't operate by hearing the Word of God. Faith operates by speaking and acting on the Word.

When you hear the Word, you believe; but when you speak and act on the Word, you receive.

If you hear the Word, but never speak and act on that Word, then the faith you received will never operate for you. Many will hear the Word preached or taught, but if they're negligent to speak and act on that Word, it won't work for them.

Many Christians don't have the things they know God has made available for them because they have been negligent to operate faith for what God's provided for them.

Although God has already provided everything for us that we will ever need spiritually, mentally, physically and materially, they won't just fall on us automatically just because they belong to us. We must exercise our faith to receive them.

God is not withholding anything from us. At the time we pray, God sends our answer, but much of what we need has to come to pass in this world where Satan is god (Second Corinthians 4:4), so he endeavors to hinder our answers from reaching us. But as we diligently exercise our faith, those hindrances of the enemy are overcome, and our answer will manifest.

Many think that if they're in the will of God, then things will automatically work for them. But even if you're in the will of God, you must exercise faith for what God has provided for you, or things won't work for you.

Hebrews 6:12 warns us, *"That ye be not slothful, but followers of them who through faith and patience inherit the promises."*

If we're slothful to exercise our faith, we won't lay hold of the promises that are ours, but if we diligently exercise our faith, speaking and acting in line with what God says is ours, we become possessors of what God has provided for us.

1 C 2:13 which things, not in words
which mans wisdom teaches,
but which the Holy Ghost teaches...

1 J 2:27 The same anointing
teaches you all things & is
truth   Rom 5³ The love of God has been
                    shed abroad in my heart by
1 Thes 4:9   you yourselves are taught
of God 2 love one another

Col 2:7 Rooted & built up in Him
& established in faith, as uv
been taught abounding therein w/
thanksgiving

2 Thes 2:15   taught traditions
                    by word
                or our epistle

Tit 1:9? read (Ex Acts 13:45; Rom 10:21)
gainsayer - 2 speak agns / contradict
2 oppose ones self 2 one
decline 2 obey him
declare ones self agns him
refuse 2v anything sd w/him

Chapter 22

SPEAKING EVIL

First Peter 3:10 instructs us, *"For he that will <u>love life</u>, and <u>see good days</u>, let him refrain his tongue from evil, and his lips that they speak no guile."*

One way we give place to the devil is by using our words to speak evil about other people. (Love thinks no evil)

* You'll never be spiritual until you learn that another man's business is not your own. It is so important that we learn to keep our mouths off other people.

Peter stated, *"For he that will love life, and <u>see good days</u>...."* A sick day is not a good day. Many don't realize that there is a direct connection between their health and the way they speak about other people. I want to love life. I want to see good days – not bad days, so I'm going to keep my words right about other people.

* God has not left you to try to rule your tongue alone, but if you will take time to speak in other tongues every day, it will help you keep your tongue under.

Jude 1:20 & 21 tells us, *"But ye, beloved, building up yourselves on your most holy faith, PRAYING IN THE HOLY GHOST, KEEP YOURSELVES IN THE LOVE OF GOD...."* Love never spoke badly of anyone. By praying in other tongues, you give place to the love of God that's in you, and that love constrains us from using our words to harm others.

Let's use our words to bless, and not to harm or injure, then we don't give place to the enemy. Let's keep our words right, and live days that are full of good things – days of heaven on earth.

Chapter 23

Dealing Honestly In Financial Matters

Another way believers can give place to the devil is by not dealing honestly and fairly in financial matters and in business dealings.

Acts 5 tells us the familiar story of what happened to Ananias and Sapphira during the early days of the church. They sold property and brought the money to give to the church. They told Peter that they were giving the entire price of the sale to the church. Now, no one told them to do that. It was their money to do with as they chose. They could have just told Peter, we're keeping a portion and we're giving a portion to the church, and that would have been fine. But they told Peter they were giving the whole amount when they weren't.

It was this lie about their giving that caused judgment to fall on them. Ananias and Sapphira both lied about the money, and both fell dead during the church service.

They tried to look big in the eyes of others through money, but it turned out badly for them.

Making It Right

Luke 19:2-9 tells us the story of Zacchaeus, who was a tax collector. Jesus came through town and He saw Zacchaeus up in a tree, who had climbed up there to get a view of Jesus. Jesus told

Zacchaeus that He was going to his house to eat with him that day.

While Jesus was at Zacchaeus' house, Zacchaeus committed to Jesus, saying, *"...Lord, the half of my goods I give to the poor; and if I have taken any thing from any man by false accusation, I restore him fourfold. And Jesus said unto him, This day is salvation come to this house...."*

Notice, when Zacchaeus set his financial dealings in proper order, Jesus said that was when salvation came to his house. Salvation didn't just come to Zacchaeus that day, but to his house, his whole family.

Many Christians don't have the blessings that Jesus provided for them operating in their lives because they don't deal honestly and fairly in money and business matters.

Aimee Semple McPherson was an evangelist in the early part of the 1900's. When she would conduct crusades in different cities, the city officials would note that as a result of her crusades, the entire economy of their city would change. The economy would improve because Sister Aimee taught the thousands of new converts to go set their financial matters in order. She taught them that if they owed something, they were to pay it, and God would help them to pay off their debts.

In fact, so great was the positive affect of Sister Aimee's crusades on a city's economy that many city officials would invite her to conduct a crusade in their city just because of the affect they knew it would have on their economy.

Jesus Took Our Place In Lack

You may have accumulated a lot of debt, but if you will exercise your faith diligently for the money you need, God will cause the money you need to meet your debts to come to you.

You may have been raised in poverty, but poverty is part of

the curse that Jesus bore for you so that you would never have to live in poverty again.

Second Corinthians 8:9 tells us, *"...though he* (Jesus) *was rich, yet for your sakes he became poor, that ye through his poverty might be rich."* "Rich" means a full supply. He has taken our place in lack so that we can have a full supply all the days of our life. But we must exercise faith every day for that supply to come to us.

No Church Deals

If we're to be upright in our business dealings, we can't be going to church with the idea of striking a business deal off the other church members.

God gathers people in the local church for His purposes, and not so men can make a buck for their business.

In Jesus' day there were people in the temple who were there just to make money, but Jesus made a whip and ran them out.

If we're to be blessed financially, we must be upright regarding financial and business matters.

Since God has provided a supply for us, we never have to slight anyone financially or in a business deal, We are to have faith that God will take care of us.

Financially Right Toward God

If we're to be upright in our finances, we must be upright financially toward God. Deuteronomy 8:18 tells us, *"But thou shalt remember the LORD thy God: for it is he that giveth thee power to get* (produce) *wealth, that he may establish his covenant...."* God gives us the power to produce wealth so that we can partner with Him financially in helping fund His work in the earth.

If we're upright financially, then we must do our part to fund the Gospel. That funding begins by faithfully giving tithes (a tenth) of all our increase to the local church, as well as giving offerings (the amount we give above the tithe).

God wants us to have all our needs supplied, but to enjoy His supply we must be doers of the Word in every arena of life – even financially.

Chapter 24

SUBMITTING TO ONE ANOTHER

One way we can give place to the devil in our life is if we fail to do what Paul instructed in Ephesians 5:21, *"Submitting yourselves one to another in the fear of God."*

Many are acquainted with the next verse in Ephesians 5:22 where Paul wrote, *"Wives, submit yourselves unto your own husbands, as unto the Lord."* This verse is meant to offer a means of protection, and it is a blessing to the wife who has a godly, loving husband who has her best interests at heart; she should have no problem submitting to a husband who treats her as the Lord would treat her.

But few are as acquainted with the previous verse (verse 21) which reads, *"Submitting yourselves one to another in the fear of God."*

The word "submit" means "willing to be led". If you're not willing to be led by someone who knows more than you, you're going to fail in life.

In a marriage, before the wife is told to submit to the husband, they are told in the previous verse to submit to one another.

What does that mean?

Every person has strengths and weaknesses. In a marriage, the husband may be strong in one area, but weak in another area. The wife may be strong in an area where the husband is weak. But the husband may be strong where the wife is weak. If that's the case, then they should submit to the strengths in one another.

If the wife is strong in dealing with the money matters, but the husband is weak in that area, then it would serve the husband well to let the wife take the lead in handling the finances. That doesn't show the husband to be weak, but it's letting the strength that's in the wife come to the front; then his weakness is covered by her strength.

Likewise, if the wife is weak in a particular area, but the husband is strong in that area, then it would work well to let the husband take the lead in that.

If you allow the strength that's in your spouse to cover for your weakness, then their strength will carry you past your weakness.

It's not a sign of weakness to let your spouse take the lead in a particular arena where you may be weak; it's actually scriptural to submit to one another.

If you're weak in a particular arena, be aware of that and draw on the strength of your spouse. Don't be defensive about a weakness you may have, but become a student to your spouse in that area and fortify yourself.

Someone may say, "Well, I'm the head of the house, so that means that I take the lead in everything." Being the head of the house doesn't mean that you get everything your way. Being the head of the house means you consider what's best for everyone in the house, and then you base your decisions on what's best for everyone. If you're head of the house, then you should be the first to see the strengths of those in your house and put their strengths to work for you. Appreciate the strengths in your spouse and of those in your household, and employ those strengths in the way that would best serve everyone in the house.

If one spouse seems to believe God easier regarding financial matters, then let that spouse take the lead in believing God for things that pertain to the finances. Now, don't misunderstand me. That doesn't dismiss the other spouse from exercising faith for finances. It just means you'll hook your faith on with the one who is taking the lead.

If the other spouse seems to believe God more easily for matters concerning healing, then let that spouse take the lead in praying if someone in the house becomes sick. Again, if you're weak in that area, that doesn't dismiss you from the need to develop your faith in that area.

When Christians don't submit to the strengths in each other, they end up fighting each other because their spouse isn't like them.

Be thankful, not threatened, by the strengths in your spouse; appreciate and submit to those strengths. When you do, you'll be the one to benefit from them.

Listen to one another, appreciate one another, submit to one another, and let your weaknesses get covered over by the strengths in each other.

As Dr. Lester Sumrall stated so well, "If those in a marriage are exactly alike, one of you is unnecessary!"

Chapter 25

YOUR GREATEST ASSET

Do you know what your greatest asset is? It's your body.

Some may say that their greatest asset is their spirit, but did you know that without a body, your spirit would have no house? Without your body, your spirit has no way to carry out the call and assignment God has placed on your life for this earth.

Your body is what gives your spirit permission to reside on this earth. Without your body, you would not be a physical being, and your spirit would have to go live in Heaven.

God has made you the steward of your body; He is not the steward of your body. He has provided healing for the body, but you are the one who must exercise faith for your body and handle it with proper care.

You cannot violate natural laws concerning the body and live in health. Faith is not so you can mishandle this wonderful machine, the body, and still expect it to work properly.

Some people don't rest properly and they run their bodies down, and start having physical problems. Then they get in a minister's healing line and want hands laid on them for healing. But to receive healing, they're going to have to make the needed corrections first. Really, it's not healing they need. They need to judge themselves on how they're handling their body, and make the needed corrections. When they do, then their faith will work so that they can receive their healing.

Every man of faith who has been an example for others to follow were not body-conscious, they were spirit-conscious. But, they did understand that God had made them stewards of their own bodies; not to serve it, but to give it proper care.

Too much of what is talked about in some circles is to make people fearful about their bodies and to make them body-conscious; and it leads them away into unbalanced teaching about health and nutrition.

The only guideline that's laid out in the New Testament for the believer is to be moderate in all things. We don't need to get off into a ditch over anything, but stay balanced and in the middle of the road.

We must be aware that as stewards of our bodies, we should give our bodies proper nutrition, exercise, and proper rest.

If we'll judge ourselves on these things, and make any needed changes, then we can live out our full length of days as we carry out God's assignment on this earth.

In Conclusion

Jesus has redeemed us from the curse, and restored to us the authority that Adam lost. Let's not give the enemy a place in us, and let's keep the door closed to him. Let's live as rich as we are, and then our days will be as days of Heaven on this earth.

BOOKS BY DR. ED DUFRESNE

Devil, Don't Touch My Stuff!
Faithfulness: The Road to Divine Promotion
Golden Nuggets for Longevity
Praying God's Word
The Footsteps of a Prophet
There's a Healer in the House
Things that Pertain to the Spirit

BOOKS BY NANCY DUFRESNE

A Supernatural Prayer Life
Daily Healing Bread from God's Table
God: The Revealer of Secrets
His Presence Shall be My Dwelling Place
Responding to the Holy Spirit
The Healer Divine
There Came a Sound from Heaven: The Life Story of Ed Dufresne
Victory in the Name
Visitations from God

For a complete list of books, CDs, and DVDs by Dr. Ed or Nancy Dufresne, or to be on the mailing list of Ed Dufresne Ministries, please contact us at:

Ed Dufresne Ministries
P.O. Box 1010
Murrieta, CA 92564

(951) 696-9258
www.eddufresne.org

- There is "the other side" of this

- Its going to all right

- Be patient in advancement

- I know exactly what the devil is trying to get me to do - open door to offense, strife hatred & bitterness

- Cast my cares upon you
- wreck my spirit